His Name Was Jesus

His Name Was Jesus

By MARY ALICE JONES

Illustrated by Rafaello Busoni

RAND McNALLY & COMPANY - Chicago
NEW YORK   SAN FRANCISCO

The author is deeply grateful for help from many sources over many years as she has studied the life of Jesus with boys and girls and their parents and teachers, and as she has continued these studies in universities and theological seminaries. It is not possible to mention by name all who have generously shared their knowledge and their faith.

But for detailed suggestions on the writing of this story of Jesus she is especially grateful to Miss Hazel A. Lewis, to Professor Martin Rist, to Dr. Roy Swim, and to Dean Luther A. Weigle. Though they are to be held in no way responsible for what is said, they graciously gave time and thoughtful attention to this writing, and offered illuminating and helpful suggestions.

Contents

Contents — continued

Introduction

JESUS is the most important person who ever lived. No one book can tell all that one wants to know about him. There are many books that may help people to know Jesus. There are churches and homes where they may learn what Jesus means to men and women and boys and girls today.

This book tells only a part of what one wants to know about Jesus. It tells the story of the life of Jesus as he lived in Palestine among the carpenters and fishermen, the housewives and children, the tax collectors and the Roman soldiers, the learned scholars and the important men of affairs, the crafty lawyers and the cruel rulers, the fiery revolutionists and the selfish collaborators, the good people and the bad people of his day.

It tells of his family, his boyhood playmates, the friends of his young manhood. It tells of his hopes for his country and his disappointments. It tells of the great crowds which gathered to listen as he traveled about the country, speaking strange new words of hope to the people of his country during the time when their land was occupied by foreign rulers. It tells of the jealousies and fears of some of his countrymen toward the Teacher whom they did not understand, and of the ways they sought to discredit him before the people. It tells of the love other people felt for him, and of their eagerness to follow him. It tells of what he taught men about God and God's way for them. It tells of the conflict between Jesus, on the one hand, and the important men of his country and the Roman officials, on the other. And it tells how that conflict ended.

This story of what Jesus did as he lived among men in Palestine is not all about Jesus. But it is a part of what one wants to know about the most important person who ever lived, the story of whose life has been called "the greatest story ever told."

MARY ALICE JONES

Evanston, Illinois

His Name Was Jesus

CHAPTER I

The Hilltop

A boy ran up the steep hill back of the village of Nazareth. Standing on the ridge, his hand made a visor to shade his eyes from the slanting rays of the late afternoon sun as he looked down on the great road, the Way of the Sea.

"There goes the caravan Simon told me about this afternoon," he said, his voice rippling with delight. "I had thought I would miss it. It must have taken a long time to pass the customhouse."

Eagerly he began counting the camels as they swung along the road toward the sea ports, their backs piled high with great bundles of goods from Damascus. "Twenty-one, twenty-two—it is a large caravan, as Simon said it was."

The sun in his face and the swaying of the huge bundles in their striped coverings made it difficult to count accurately. To rest his eyes, the boy Jesus looked for a moment toward the north where the high mountains rose, snow-capped Hermon towering above them all. When he turned again to the caravan, he laughed to see a few little donkeys trailing along almost hidden by their loads.

Suddenly he heard sharper hoofbeats. Sweeping around the hill from the east came two chariots followed by a band of

Roman soldiers, their spears and shields flashing in the sunlight. Jesus saw the caravan hurriedly move off the road to make way for the passage of the foreign soldiers. For a moment the joy went out of the day, as he was reminded that his beloved land of Israel was no longer a free country. He was sad as he watched the soldiers pass on ahead of the caravan while the camels and the donkeys staggered back onto the great road.

Then he whirled around and looked south. "It will not always be so," he said confidently. "Here is the plain of Esdraelon, peopled with the heroes of my own country. I will not think of the Roman conquerors, but of the greatness of Israel." His face was happy again as he remembered that beyond Esdraelon lay the Great City. It was too far away to be seen from the hilltop. But Jesus knew it was there, and just to look toward it made his heart beat faster. Jerusalem, the city of great King David of old! The Holy City of his people—how often he had dreamed of it! And now he was going to see it. In the morning he would be on his way to the great celebration of his nation, the Passover festival at Jerusalem.

He scrambled over the rocks to his favorite spot, a circle of green grass pierced by red anemones, with a boulder in the center. Since he had been big enough to climb the hill, Jesus had loved to come to this spot. Something exciting could be seen in all directions. But now he turned away from the caravan moving westward toward the land of the conquerors. To the north the setting sun was painting the snow on Mount Hermon with glowing colors. To the east the long shadows of the orchards and vineyards, the groves and fields of grain in the fertile province of Galilee, were merging with the shadows of the hills to hide the Sea of Galilee and the Jordan River. But it was toward the south that he wanted to look longest; so he wiggled himself into a comfortable position against the boulder and let his eyes move over the whole familiar scene. He sighed contentedly.

"Now I can think about the trip tomorrow. Think about it all I want to."

He had been busy all day. In the house his mother, Mary, had been working hard to get the food prepared for the journey and the younger children in the home ready to be left with the neighbors. And in the carpenter shop Joseph was finishing work which must be delivered before they left. Jesus had helped them both.

Just before the sunset, Joseph had looked up from the oxen yoke on which he was putting the last smoothing touches.

"The yoke is almost finished, Son," he said. "It will be ready when Samuel drives his oxen over. Everything else we promised has been delivered except these small stools for Miriam's house. James and Joses are big enough to take them so short a distance. They have been playing all the day." The carpenter had put his hand on the boy's shoulder. "But you have been working hard. You need to be out-of-doors before you go to bed, else the excitement about tomorrow will keep you awake. Run along for a while before Mother calls us to supper."

The boy had given a glad little shout and run toward the door. "There is just time to get to the top of the hill before the sun goes down," he had called over his shoulder, and away he had gone, his brown legs flashing beneath his short tunic.

Now he sat on the hilltop, thinking about tomorrow. It had seemed as if the day would never come. For weeks he had been checking off the days with red chalk on a smooth board in the carpenter shop. This morning he had checked off the last day. Only one night's sleep, and then would come the day to start.

"I am twelve years old. I am a Son of the Law. Now I am old enough to go to the great Temple with the men," he thought joyously, letting pictures of the splendid Temple float through his mind. "I wonder how many other boys will be there. Boys who will be coming for the first time, like me. Boys from all over Israel. Boys even from the lands of the Dispersion, far away, coming to Jerusalem for the Passover." His eyes sparkled. How exciting it would be to be in Jerusalem for the festival!

The boy had long known about the Passover. At home every year his family had observed it. Following the custom, Jesus would rise from the table at the proper time and ask Joseph to tell them why they celebrated this day. And Joseph would tell of the time when the families of Israel had been living as slaves in Egypt, and how God had saved them from the wicked plan of the king to keep the Israelites forever in bondage. At the synagogue school, too, the boys had been taught carefully by the old rabbi. So Jesus had heard the story of the Passover again and again. Now he would take part in the ceremonies in Jerusalem.

"The great teachers will be there, too," he was remembering. "Our rabbi says they are the wisest men in all our nation. I shall listen to them as they teach in the court of the Temple." His thoughts ran on. "There is so much the rabbi has not taught us. I want to know why God does not set us free from the Roman conquerors and make us a great nation again as we were under King David. I want to know more about the Messiah promised to save our nation, and when he is to come."

A noise broke his thoughts. He jumped up and saw Simon, a boy his own age, climbing the hill. "Did you know I was up here?" Jesus called.

Simon reached the top as he answered. "Yes, Joseph told me." He looked quickly over the road. "You did see the caravan, didn't you?" he began. Then he stopped, and went on almost angrily. "But you have forgotten the caravan. You have been thinking those deep thoughts of yours again. I see it in your eyes."

"You always seem angry when I think about things, Simon. Why do you?"

"We're different, that's all." Then Simon added, "You pay attention better, too, and learn more when the rabbi teaches us." As if ashamed of paying a compliment, he quickly picked up a stone and sent it hurtling down the hillside. The movement seemed to give him confidence. "But when it comes to aiming stones, I can beat you any day. Watch!"

He selected a smooth stone with care, then stood looking over the hillside. "See that bush away down there? The big one with the yellow flowers?" Jesus nodded. "I'll send this stone straight into it. Just with my hand; without a slingshot." He stood poised for a moment against the western sky, red with sunset. Then he raised his arm and let go. The stone flew straight toward the bush, broke through its leaves and landed with a thud on the ground among the roots, sending up a spray of loose earth and gravel.

"Good, Simon! That was good! How do you do it?"

"Oh, a steady eye and arm and a little practice are all it takes," Simon answered smugly. "You could do it, I suppose, if you tried." He looked up to see his friend's eyes twinkling, as he made a swinging movement pantomiming a hand planing a board. Simon remembered that Jesus worked in a carpenter shop where a steady arm and eye were needed. He returned a grin for the twinkle. "You are pretty good with your hands yourself when you forget your thinking," he admitted. "But this hilltop does set you off." As Simon looked south, over the plain of Esdraelon, it seemed that he himself was lost in thought for a moment. He turned sud-

15

denly. His face was stern as he pointed toward Esdraelon.

"Over there on the plain is where our forefathers fought. They fought, and they won. But what do we do? We pay taxes to the cursed publicans!" He spoke the word in scorn. "Outcasts of Israel who collect taxes for the Romans so the conquerors can keep their soldiers on our roads and their puppet kings ruling over us." He picked up another stone and threw it, not carefully aimed this time, but fiercely. "We are fools and cowards."

"I wonder and wonder about it, too, Simon."

"Wonder about it? That's the trouble with us. We wonder about it instead of doing something about it."

"What should we do? We have no soldiers. And besides—"

"Maybe we don't have soldiers, but we have men," Simon retorted. "Why don't they fight as our forefathers fought when the Philistines and the Assyrians and the Macedonians came against our country? If we only had a leader! Like King David." His voice sank lower. "Or like Judas Maccabaeus."

"The rabbi says God will save us in his own good time."

Simon's face was gloomy. "I know, I know," he said wearily. He was silent for a moment. Then he seemed to make up his mind. "You can keep a secret, so I will tell you." He spoke in a whisper, though there was no one else to hear. "Some of the men *are* going to fight. They have a secret underground organization. They call themselves the Zealots."

Jesus was startled. "Are you sure?"

Simon nodded. "My brother Amos knows some of the men. They are gathering arms and hiding them. They have secret meetings. They are sending messengers to other towns in Galilee. It won't be long now, before they are ready."

He straightened up. He forgot caution as his voice rose. "Then the Romans will know that the men of Israel are not afraid. They will fight for their freedom and they will win."

17

"But, Simon, God has promised to send the Messiah to save us."

"Maybe the Messiah is here now, waiting for the men of Israel to show that they are worthy of him. Maybe as soon as we prove ourselves ready, he will make himself known. Then he will set up the throne of David and once more we shall be a great nation."

Jesus turned again toward the south. "You can't see beyond Esdraelon, where the battles were fought, Simon. But Jerusalem is beyond the plain, and the Temple of God is there. Maybe God has another way to save us. Maybe the Messiah won't need armies."

"There you go, dreaming again. How can we be saved from Roman soldiers except by fighting them? I tell you, we've got to fight. And I'm going to be in the battle. If I'm old enough to be a Son of the Law, I'm old enough to fight."

Jesus tossed his head as if to clear his mind.

"Maybe when we are at Jerusalem the teachers will tell us more about it. Why God lets the Romans rule over us now, and how God will deliver us."

Simon's anger seemed to die away. "I wish they would," he said wistfully. "Maybe when we get to the Temple it will all seem different."

"I'm sure it will, Simon." Jesus' eyes were shining now. "Think of it! Tomorrow we are going to the Temple—you and I and other boys from all over Israel! As soon as we have had supper and have gone to sleep we shall wake up and it will be the day to start."

Simon, too, was excited over the thought of going to the Great City. But he was less ready to admit it. He started down the hill. "Well, right now I'm interested in supper."

With a last look at the road over which he would travel, Jesus ran after him. An hour later both boys were sound asleep.

CHAPTER II

Along the Winding Road

B<small>EFORE</small> dawn the next day, the town of Nazareth was full of bustle. Last-minute preparations were made, breakfast was eaten, provisions and tents were loaded on the donkeys, and just as the sun came up over the eastern ridge, the people of the town who were going to the festival were on their way.

The boys hurried along ahead of the others. What would be around the next bend in the road? And the next? But the sun was hot and the road was dusty. By-and-by the boys grew tired. They dropped back with their families.

Mary, who was riding on the donkey, looked down at her son. "The last time you and I came along this road, you were riding on the donkey with me," she reminded him.

The boy laughed. "And wouldn't it look funny if I should ride with you now?" he bantered. "Of course, it was all right for a baby to ride, even if he was a boy."

The mother seemed to be thinking aloud. "That was a wonderful trip, Son. You were born while we were away."

Glancing up merrily the boy asked, "And what is so wonderful about my being born, Mother? Babies are born every day."

His mother returned his smile, but in her heart she knew

that her son was the most wonderful baby ever to be born.

Joseph's voice broke into her thoughts. "We shall stop to rest around this bend," he said. As he spoke, the donkey rounded a curve in the road, and they saw a pleasant stream just to one side, running among the myrtle bushes, with taller sycamore trees along the bank.

Quickly the Nazareth group gathered in the shade of the trees. The women began to prepare the meal, the men sat on the ground talking, and the boys ran to the stream, untied their sandals, tucked their striped coats into their girdles, and dashed into the cool water.

All too soon the rest period was over, and the travelers were again on the road. Just before dark they came to a good camping place, and stopped for the night. When supper had been eaten, the food was cleared away carefully lest any remaining bits attract the wolves and wild dogs. Then the women went to rest under the tents which had been set up for them, and the men and boys gathered round the fire.

"Tell us about the great battles of Israel," Simon asked the rabbi. "When Saul killed his thousands and David his tens of thousands."

The rabbi hesitated. Then he spoke kindly. "We are going to the Temple to remember God's goodness to Israel, Simon. Would it not be more fitting to hear how Moses brought our fathers through the wilderness to the Promised Land?"

Simon wanted to hear about battles, but he knew he must not argue with the rabbi. "You know best, Rabbi," he said respectfully. And as they all became still, the old rabbi told once again the story that all the boys and most of the men had heard him tell again and again at the synagogue school in Nazareth. But so vividly did he tell it that not one of them failed to listen. Each one felt again the thrill of high joy in the remembrance of the courage of the great leader, Moses,

and of the continuing care of their God, even during the dreary days of hunger and thirst in the hot, barren land through which their forefathers had wandered so long.

After the story was finished, Amos, Simon's older brother, broke the silence. "Rabbi, why does not God again deliver us? Why does he allow Rome to hold us in bondage?"

The old man looked troubled. But this time he did not hesitate. He knew what lay back of the question. He had heard rumors of the activity of the Zealots. "My son, be not deceived. They are false prophets who would call you to take God's affairs into your own hands. Wait patiently for him. He will bring our deliverance to pass in his own good time."

Joseph's face was serious in the firelight. "The rabbi speaks wise counsel, Amos," he said quietly. "It would be folly to take the sword against Rome." And many of the older men nodded in agreement. Amos was silenced. But the boy Jesus, watching the circle about the fire, noticed that some of the young men were not convinced. They looked away from the older men and toward one another as if they shared a secret which they dared not tell their elders.

The day had been long and the men were all tired. The old rabbi repeated the evening prayer, and one by one the men and boys each found a place on the ground which suited him best, wrapped his cloak around him and lay down to rest.

Simon motioned to Jesus to come to a place a little apart from the others. "I have something to tell you," he whispered.

When the two boys were lying side by side, Simon spoke in an excited undertone. "Some of the young men right here are members of the Zealots." He heard the sharply drawn breath of his friend. "They are going to meet others when the groups from beyond Jordan join us tomorrow."

"How do you know, Simon?"

Simon thought a moment before he answered. "I can trust

you. I wouldn't tell any of the other boys." His voice sank lower still. "Amos is a Zealot."

Though he was not so surprised as his friend had thought he would be, Jesus was troubled. Simon chattered on, full of his own ideas of what the daring plans of the young men might be. But Jesus scarcely listened. He had known Amos all his life. As one of the older boys at the synagogue school in Nazareth, Amos had set the others an example of respect for the rabbi. Yet now he was breaking away. Against the advice of the older men, he was joining the underground army pledged to fight Rome. Could it be that the rabbi and Joseph were wrong?

By-and-by Simon's voice became blurred, then ceased as he dropped off to sleep.

But Jesus went on thinking, his eyes fixed on the distant stars. The words he had learned at the synagogue came to him.

"The heavens declare the glory of God
And the firmament showeth his handiwork.
The law of the Lord is perfect,
The commandment of the Lord is pure,
The judgments of the Lord are true and righteous
          altogether.
More to be desired are they than gold,
And in keeping of them there is great
          reward."

"The rabbi is right," he thought. "God must be the judge. He knows what is best for Israel. If we trust him, our nation will get its reward."

And so, comforted, he fell asleep.

The next day pilgrims from other towns joined the Nazareth group, and there was a great crowd on the road to Jerusalem. As old friends greeted each other after long separations, and as the leaders sought to keep the people all moving

23

along, there was a constant shifting back and forth among the throng. All day Simon was watching the young men to see if he could recognize the Zealots from the other towns. Toward evening he reported to Jesus that he knew Amos had talked with some of them.

"But I think they have decided to wait a while before doing anything," he added, a note of disappointment in his voice. "I had thought they might have a battle in Jerusalem during the Passover."

"Oh, no, Simon! Not during the festival!"

"Why not? That would be the best time. The people are there from all over the country. I know they would all fight, once someone started the battle. That is all they need. Just someone to start the fighting."

"Have you forgotten that the Romans send extra soldiers to Jerusalem during the Passover?" Jesus asked. "They are always prepared for trouble at festival times. The tower of Antonia is full of soldiers, and they pace the wall of the city. The men of Nazareth have told us about it every year when they have returned from Jerusalem." He touched Simon lightly on the shoulder. "Come, forget about fighting. We will be in the Great City ourselves tomorrow. Think about that for a while."

The next day the pilgrims did come to Jerusalem. When they first saw the city, high on a hill, the great dome of the Temple shining in the afternoon sun, the old men wiped the tears from their eyes and thanked God that once more they had been permitted to see the Holy City. The boys were so full of excitement that they could scarcely remember that they were now Sons of the Law, and must not shout and dance as children would have done. The faces of the young men, even those who had thought the rabbi was wrong, lighted up as they looked toward the Temple.

24

The rabbi gathered the crowd about him and began singing the familiar song of ascents:

"I will lift up mine eyes unto the hills.
From whence cometh my help?"

And the people responded joyously:

"My help cometh from the Lord
Which made heaven and earth."

The rabbi continued:

"He will not suffer thy foot to stumble;
He that keepeth thee shall not slumber;

And the people answered:

"Behold, he that keepeth Israel
Shall neither slumber nor sleep."

Again the rabbi spoke:

"The Lord is thy keeper,
The Lord is thy shade
Upon thy right hand."

And the people:

"The sun shall not smite thee by day,
Nor the moon by night."

Then came the words of the rabbi:

"The Lord shall preserve thee from all evil,
He shall preserve thy soul."

And the glad affirmation:

"The Lord shall preserve
Thy going out and thy coming in
From this time forth, and even forevermore."

Jesus wanted this minute to last forever. He looked at Simon, his eyes asking the question. "How can you think of battles, Simon? We are here! In Jerusalem!"

Soon the rabbi was leading the people up the hill. The city would be crowded. The high moment passed, and the people began to think about food and shelter for the night.

CHAPTER III

The Great City

Early the next morning, Jesus and Simon hurried to the Temple. For a long while they stood outside its encircling wall, gazing at the great building. In all their dreams of the Temple they had never imagined it could be so large and so beautiful. Now that they actually were seeing it, they could hardly believe their eyes. The towering gates, opening through the surrounding wall; the courts beyond rising in terraces, each enclosed in great pillars; and finally, the white marble walls of the Temple itself soaring to its golden dome—the boys could scarcely see it all for marveling.

Timidly they passed through the south gate and entered the outer court. What a crowd there was! Men and boys from all parts of Israel, pilgrims from distant lands, men leading animals for the sacrifices, Levites bearing sacred vessels, and priests on their way to the inner courts, their robes girded with violet, purple, and scarlet sashes.

Making their way through the throng, Jesus and Simon came to a quieter place between the great pillars surrounding the court. There were many people here, too, but they were listening eagerly to one who was speaking. Coming nearer, the boys saw that a small group of older men were seated in the midst of the crowd. They were dignified and serious.

"There are the teachers," Jesus said eagerly. "We can hear if we stand on the edge of the crowd." And he hurried forward. Simon would have preferred seeing more of the vast Temple, but he knew that he could not persuade his friend to go one more step, now that he had found the teachers; so both boys joined the group.

The teachers were answering questions, explaining the sacred Law of Israel to the people. As the boys came up, someone was asking about the Sabbath. "The Law says we must do no work on the Sabbath, Rabbi," the questioner was saying. "And we know this is right. But what shall we do about our cattle? Must they fast on the Sabbath? Or should we lead them to water and feed them? Which must a man do if he would keep the law of the Sabbath, Rabbi?"

There was a moment of silence as the teachers consulted with one another about the right answer. Then one of them spoke. "My son, God is a just God. Dumb animals cannot know the Law. And so it need not be binding upon them. It is right that you give them water and food on the Sabbath."

The answer was pleasing to the people. They wanted to keep the Law, but they wanted to protect their cattle, too. They nodded and smiled. "A very wise teacher," someone near Jesus said. "A very learned rabbi."

Another question came. "Rabbi, is it lawful to eat an egg that has been laid on the Sabbath?"

There was a long discussion among the teachers. One of them answered that it was lawful, but it was clear that some of the others did not agree.

"And if one is sick, Rabbi, may a doctor be called to attend him on the Sabbath?"

The answer was carefully guarded. "If death threatens, a physician may be called," the rabbis said, adding sternly, "but only if death threatens. A broken bone may not be set, and no oil may be poured on a wound or water on a sprained foot."

It seemed very important to the teachers that the Sabbath law be kept perfectly, that no exception be made. "The Sabbath is holy," they continued solemnly, "holy unto our God. Let all true sons of Israel regard it so, lest we become as the heathen nations."

Jesus and Simon listened as more and more questions were asked. The people asked about laws concerning food. Was this food forbidden? Was that permitted? They asked about washing the hands before meals. How many times must they be washed? Was it enough to wash to the wrists or must they wash to the elbows? They asked about associating with men outside their faith, the Gentiles. Of course, they knew they must not eat with Gentiles because they ate forbidden food. But was it permitted to buy from them and to sell to them? They asked about the sacrifices to be offered at the Temple, and the sort of coins they must use to pay their Temple tax.

Jesus was feeling disappointed.

"Why do the teachers spend so much time answering these questions?" he said to Simon. "I wish they would talk about what God wants us to do to get ready for the Messiah."

"I wish they would talk about how God is going to save our nation from the Romans," Simon responded impatiently. "Come on, let's do something else. We can ask all these questions of the rabbi at home."

But Jesus wanted to stay. Maybe someone would ask the important questions. "You go on, Simon. I think I shall stay a while." But though he listened until the people went away to eat their noonday meal, he did not hear the questions he wanted answered.

There was much to see in the Great City, and every day Jesus and the other boys spent some time walking about the streets, gazing in wonder at the people from the distant lands, the strange fruits in the markets, the bazaars filled with gleaming silk and rich ornaments of gold and silver from far countries. Sweet-smelling ointments sent out perfume to mingle with the sharper odors of the herbs from the apothecary shop. Merchants and peddlers and importers were shouting their wares noisily, urging the pilgrims to buy. The boys from the little town of Nazareth went from one street to another, fascinated by the strange sights and smells and sounds.

Late one afternoon they were walking in the southwestern part of the city, among the fine houses of the wealthy families of Jerusalem and the great public buildings. As they passed the palace where the high priest of the Temple lived, men were coming out of the gate, richly dressed in beautiful coats and turbans, some of red, some of purple, some woven in stripes. The boys stood close against the wall to watch.

"Who are they?" one of the boys whispered. "They look like important men."

"I know." Another boy was speaking softly. "They are members of the Sanhedrin."

"To think that I should see members of the Sanhedrin," the first boy murmured. "The supreme court of our country! Why, the Sanhedrin can do anything."

Simon was scowling, but he, too, kept his voice low. "The Sanhedrin had real authority once. But when the Romans made Herod their puppet king, he took over even the Sanhedrin." His face was scornful as he added, "Maybe that is why they called him Herod the Great. Well, being called 'the great' didn't keep him from going mad and dying and having his kingdom divided among his sons."

"Sh-h." Several of the boys looked about fearfully. "The palace Herod built is just a little way up the hill, and the

Roman governor may have spies about," one of them breathed in Simon's ear. Then, as if to prove to anyone listening that they were merely seeing Jerusalem, he spoke aloud. "Come on. Let's see Herod's palace, where the Roman governor is staying. My uncle says it is the biggest palace in all Jerusalem."

At that moment, a group of Roman soldiers marched by, their armor glinting in the sun, their red capes swinging in rhythm with their steps. The boys stood aside, close together, saying nothing until the soldiers were out of hearing. As Jesus watched the proud conquerors, he understood more fully than he had before why Amos and the other young men were feeling so angry. Roman soldiers in the streets of the capital of their country! The city of David! The city where the Temple stood!

The boys went on up the hill, but much of the excitement had gone out of their day. They felt uneasy, as if they must watch their words carefully lest someone overhear them. They were near Herod's palace now, but they could not enjoy seeing its magnificence.

Simon's face was threatening. Jesus put his hand on his friend's arm. Simon jerked away. "If I could see the Roman beast who lives there, I would spit on him. Yes, I would. Even if he killed me, I would be glad I had done it. I hate him!"

"Simon!" The voice of Jesus was so sharp that Simon stood still, staring. He had never heard his friend speak so. Jesus spoke calmly now. "Let's go back to the others. It's almost sunset, and time for the Passover supper."

Simon's face did not clear, but as the others turned he joined them. "All right, I will go with you. But don't think you have made me stop hating him, because you haven't."

"I do not like having Roman governors rule over Jerusalem and Roman soldiers in the streets any more than you do, Simon," Jesus said quietly. "I am patriotic, too. But spitting

at a Roman governor isn't going to free us from Rome, you know. It will only get you arrested."

The boys had little to say on the way back. As they came again to the market place, Simon stopped. He looked ashamed. "I know I was silly back there." He scuffed the dust with his sandal a moment. Then he straightened up. "But what can we do? I thought the teachers might tell us something. But all they talk about is laws, laws, laws. Oh, I'm sorry again. I didn't mean to speak ill of the teachers. I know they are wise men and good. But I want to know what to do about important things."

"So do I, Simon," Jesus began thoughtfully. Then he spoke positively. "And tomorrow I am going to ask the teachers."

"What! You mean you are going to speak to the great teachers yourself?"

"Yes, I am. And I think they will listen, too. Maybe they will be glad to talk about important things."

The boys had come now to the part of the city where their lodgings were. So they said good night and each one joined his own parents. All over Jerusalem that night family groups ate the Passover supper together.

The next day, Jesus went early to the Temple. He was there when the teachers came. They looked surprised to see a boy so early, but one of them gave him a friendly smile. "Did you want to ask a question, my son?"

"Yes, Rabbi. I want to talk about the most important laws. There are so many. What are the most important ones?"

The teachers looked at one another. What a strange question for a boy to ask. Surely all the laws of Israel were important. One had to obey every one. Only so would Israel keep herself separate from the Roman conquerors and the heathen nations all about her. But as the teachers thought a moment, there was a shadow of doubt in their faces.

The friendly rabbi leaned forward. "Yes, my son, there are some laws more important than others. The first great commandment is that men should love God with their whole heart and mind and strength. And the second one is that men should love their neighbors as themselves."

Jesus felt happy now. The teachers did think other matters were more important than all the little laws the people had been asking about! At least this teacher did. But as the boy looked up eagerly, he saw that some of the teachers were not altogether pleased with the answer the friendly rabbi had given. They had begun talking among themselves. A crowd was gathering. The rabbi shook his head slightly. "Come back tomorrow after the people have gone," he said softly. So Jesus slipped away and went into the inner court of the Temple where the priests were offering the sacrifices.

The next day was the last day of the festival. The great days were almost over. Already the people were beginning to think about the business they had left undone back in their own towns. They must be on their way home. But Jesus was thinking only of the invitation of the rabbi. As he came to the pillars where the teachers were, he was glad to see that most of the people had left. He walked nearer, and the friendly rabbi nodded a welcome.

Thus it was that Jesus had the opportunity to talk with the great teachers. For soon the other teachers, as well as the friendly rabbi, were interested in the eager questions of this boy from Nazareth. They learned that he had been well taught in his own home and by the old rabbi in his own synagogue. They were surprised to find a boy who had been thinking so much about important matters. And so they were willing to stay after all the others had left to talk with him.

Time passed, and neither the boy nor the teachers thought of being hungry or sleepy.

In the meantime, the group from Nazareth was ready to start home. Joseph and Mary packed their provisions, loaded the little donkey, and joined the others from Nazareth.

"The boys have gone on ahead," a neighbor told them. And so they made their way down the hill, turned for a parting look at the Great City, and took the winding road toward Nazareth.

But the boy Jesus was not with the other boys. "When the boys were ready to start ahead, Jesus did not come," Simon told Mary and Joseph. "We thought he was with you."

"Come, we must return to the city," Joseph said, his voice troubled. "The boy cannot travel so far alone."

Mary was frightened. "How did he get lost from the others? Something must have happened to him."

"He is a strong boy, Mary. And we can trust him."

As Mary and Joseph came again to the city, it was not a joyous entrance, but one full of anxiety. They wandered about the streets, asking this person and that one if he had seen the boy. "He loves the Temple so," Joseph remembered. "Perhaps he has gone there."

Thus they found him. For a moment they stood in the shadow of the pillars without speaking. Relief flowed over them like comforting water after a dusty journey.

Then Mary forgot everything else except that her son was safe. She ran forward with a little cry. "Oh, Son, we have looked for you everywhere!"

Jesus turned toward her. He seemed surprised that Mary and Joseph had been anxious about him. "But, Mother, why didn't you come to the Temple first of all?" he asked gently. "Did you not know I would be here?"

Then he thanked the teachers and joined Joseph and Mary to return home to Nazareth.

CHAPTER IV

In the Carpenter Shop

ALONG the road going back to Nazareth the other boys were asking each other where Jesus could be. Simon looked worried. "Do you suppose one of the soldiers heard what I said about the governor and thought it was Jesus talking? Could he have been arrested?"

The other boys told Simon they were sure Jesus had not been arrested, but every few minutes during the next day they looked uneasily back over the road. About sunset one of them called, "There! There come three travelers." A moment later they recognized their neighbors.

Simon's face showed his relief. Now that he knew his friend was safe, he tried to pass his fear off lightly. "Well, it surely did take them a long time to overtake us."

The boys were surprised when they heard that Jesus had stayed so long in the Temple to talk with the teachers.

"You always were one for serious questions and deep thoughts," Simon said, half teasingly, half in earnest.

The old rabbi was amazed. "The great teachers are so busy during the festival. Why did they stay so long with you?"

Jesus could only say that they had been kind to him. He seemed not to want to talk about it.

But after he was back in Nazareth, he thought about it a great deal. The rabbis had been kind. As they had talked about God's love and his righteousness, Jesus had listened eagerly. But much that they said had seemed so far away from the questions that were most real to him. "Obey the Law," was their answer to almost all questions.

When he had asked how the people should get ready for the coming of the Messiah, the answer had been the same. "Obey the Law." And they would tell of special ways of doing everyday things, like preparing the fish and making the bread, and about special fasts and special prayers, which would cause the people of Israel to be more holy and righteous than other people, and so more pleasing to God.

When Jesus had asked how God was going to deliver Israel from the Romans, the rabbis had seemed annoyed. "That is God's affair," they answered. "It is our affair to see that we keep our synagogues, our Temple, and our religious laws safe from Roman meddling. That we observe the laws and customs which keep us separate from the heathen peoples about us."

As he thought of these things, Jesus said over and over to himself, "There is so much more men need to understand." So he studied with the old rabbi of Nazareth and learned what the prophets and the wise men of old had said. And often he went up to the hilltop by himself and asked God to help him know all he needed to know to answer his own questions.

During the months that followed that first trip to Jerusalem, Jesus was busy in the carpenter shop, too. There was much building going on in Galilee. Near Nazareth the Romans were rebuilding Sepphoris, a great city which had been destroyed in an uprising a few years before. And not far away, Herod Antipas was building a new city to be called

Tiberias in honor of the Roman emperor, Tiberius Caesar. Joseph had more work than usual because the Romans had come through the country recruiting workers, and many of the younger carpenters and joiners and masons of Galilee had gone to work on the new cities.

When Simon heard that men of Nazareth were working for the Romans he was furious. He came to the carpenter shop, almost shouting in his anger. "They are traitors to work for the Romans! Traitors—just as the publicans are who collect taxes for them!"

After Simon had left, Jesus talked with Joseph about it.

"Why do the men work for the Romans when they hate them so? They are not made to go, are they?"

"No, the Romans have not yet made us slaves," Joseph answered. "But I think, perhaps, we are making ourselves slaves."

"Making ourselves slaves?"

"Yes, Son, slaves to Mammon. Slaves to money. The Romans pay higher wages than the people can earn in their own villages."

"But how can they work for the Romans? Won't they be despised by their neighbors?"

Joseph put aside the board which he was smoothing. His face was deeply lined and very pale. In quick concern Jesus forgot about his neighbors and the Romans.

"You are sick, Father. Here, let me help you. Lie down on the bench." Joseph allowed the boy to help him and for a moment he rested, his eyes closed. Then he roused himself. "It is nothing. It will pass. I will rest a moment longer."

Jesus watched anxiously, wondering if he should call Mary. Just as he had decided that he must call her, Joseph raised up on his elbow. "You were asking about our men working for the Romans, Son. Yes, it is going to make bad feeling in the town. Some of the workers say it is right to get as much money as we can from the Romans. Others, like Simon, say it is being a traitor to work for them. But the Pharisees, who know our Law better than common people do, say it is wicked to have any dealing with the Romans or to touch their money, because they worship idols."

He paused as if to arrange his thoughts carefully before expressing them. "You know there are Zealots here in Nazareth."

Jesus nodded and Joseph went on. "They are the young, hot-headed ones, plotting a war with Rome. But the party of the Pharisees and the scribes, the good citizens and the teachers, are trying to be neutral about Rome. They say we should think only of obeying God's laws for Israel, and leave the Romans to God."

"Yes, that is what the teachers in the Temple said," Jesus remembered.

Joseph rested a moment before he went on. "Israel herself is divided, Son. Even her leaders disagree among themselves." As if it was hard for him to bring himself to say it, he added sadly, "Many members of the party of the Sadducees are working with the Roman officials."

"The Sadducees? Why, the high priest of the Temple and many of the members of the Sanhedrin are Sadducees. Can such men be working with the conquerors of their country?"

"Yes, Son. It is true. I had heard rumors before. But when we were in Jerusalem I heard it said plainly. Herod the Great gave much money to build the beautiful Temple. That was to keep our people quiet. Then he and the Romans appointed as high priests men who would work with them. And so it continues today."

There was shocked silence while the boy tried to understand. "Do you mean that the high priests accept appointments from Romans? From pagans who do not even believe in our God?"

"The Sadducees are rich and prominent and want to keep their money and their power. Only the Romans can reward them with the appointment to high office."

"Surely not all our leaders are traitors, Father. Most of them are good Israelites, aren't they?"

Joseph smiled sadly. "Probably none of them thinks he is a traitor, Son. Each one probably has persuaded himself that what he is doing is best for the country as well as best for himself." He paused a moment. "But no, you are right. Not all our leaders seek favor with the Romans. Only a few of the Sadducees actually collaborate with the Romans, and the Pharisees say they are unclean if they touch a Roman."

"But who is right? The Zealots want to fight. The Sadducees, you say, want to work with the Romans because it gives them money and power. And the Pharisees keep away from them altogether. Who is right?"

The lines on Joseph's face seemed to deepen. "I do not know, Son. I do not know. I am only a carpenter. I cannot understand all these things. When our leaders and teachers are divided, it is a sad day for Israel."

The carpenter shop was very quiet. So quiet that the wind in the leaves of the fig trees outside the window rustled noisily, and the sound came clearly of the grinding of one stone upon another as women crushed their grain in a neighboring yard.

When Joseph spoke again his voice was low but confident. "God has not deserted us. God will be with his people, Israel. 'Hear, O Israel, the Lord thy God is one God. And thou shalt love the Lord thy God with all thy heart and all thy soul and all thy strength.'"

As the solemn words he had heard so often were spoken, Jesus stood up as he had been taught, and faced toward the

Holy City. When he turned again, Joseph seemed strangely still. Hurriedly the boy came to the bench. He saw that Joseph was very ill.

Though he grew better in the following weeks, Joseph was never strong again. More and more he entrusted to Jesus the work in the carpenter shop.

There was less time, now, for climbing the hill and watching the road. There was less time, too, for talks with the other boys as Jesus worked day after day at the carpenter bench. Joseph had taught him well, and he took pride in his work. He was teaching the younger boys, too, and James and Joses were learning rapidly. And so the boy Jesus grew up.

A few years later, Joseph, the beloved carpenter of Nazareth, died. The neighbors and the rabbi were kind and did all they could to help. But Jesus knew that now he must take the father's place in the family. He must work hard to take care of his mother and the younger children in their home.

Simon came to the carpenter shop almost every day. He seemed to feel that he had to talk with Jesus about the Zealots, though he knew his friend felt the Zealots were wrong.

"You know the history of Israel better than I do," Simon said one day. "Why don't you see that we can never be free unless we fight the Romans?"

"You think that if we fight the Romans we will win, Simon. Joseph thought we would not win, and I think he was right. The Roman legions are too strong for us."

"But—"

"No, wait a minute," Jesus went on, as Simon started to interrupt. "You will say that it is better to fight for freedom and lose than not to fight at all. But there must be a better way to overcome Roman cruelty than by more cruelty." His face was serious but eager, too. "Think of this: maybe God will show Israel the better way. When the Messiah comes it will all be clear to us. God has not deserted Israel. Of that I am sure."

Simon was not convinced. Though he loved him, he thought Jesus was a dreamer.

Just at daybreak one spring morning, Jesus was awakened by hearing someone walking stealthily up the outside stairway of the house. As he got up to see who the intruder was, a tall figure came onto the roof where Jesus had his pallet, and he recognized Simon. "Come down quietly. Don't wake the others. I have something to tell you."

A moment later they were standing together in Mary's little garden.

"I am telling no one else," Simon began, "but I had to tell you." He took a deep breath. Then he spoke firmly. "I have joined the Zealots."

In the gray dawn, the two friends faced each other for a long moment. The birds were waking up now, and the cooing doves and chirping sparrows and cawing crows flew over their heads. Farther away hungry dogs were howling. But the two youths heard nothing. They were absorbed in their own thoughts.

Simon broke the silence. "I am off today—now—for a near-by city." He hesitated, then added, "In fact—for Sepphoris."

"Sepphoris? You mean—?"

"Yes, I am going to take work there. I am sent as a spy. I am to find out how many soldiers there are and where they are stationed. We are going to fight there—soon."

"Simon," Jesus began. Then he stopped. He wanted to try to persuade his friend not to go. Yet he knew he could not persuade him. It seemed that he had to go. "I know you are doing what you think is right, Simon. God bless you and keep you."

"And God bless you and keep you," Simon responded

solemnly. "I know you are doing what you think is right, too."

· So Simon went off with the Zealots, and Jesus, heavy-hearted, went back to the carpenter shop.

Many people in Nazareth noticed that Simon and Amos and some of the other young men of Nazareth had gone away. It was said they had gone away to work. Their friends thought they knew why they had left, but they did not talk about it. They knew it must be kept secret.

But some of the men of Nazareth who had been working for the Romans were uneasy. Not many days later at Sepphoris, one of them caught sight of Simon working in the city. Simon, who had been heard to say he would have no dealings with the Romans except in battle!

"What is he doing here?" the man asked a neighbor. It did not take the men long to make up their minds. "Simon has joined the Zealots," they agreed. Looking at one another, their faces strained, one of them added, "And the Zealots must have made a plot against the Romans here."

After a moment his neighbor put their fear into words. "If he is caught, we shall probably be thought guilty, too, because we are from his town." He shuddered. "The Romans are not gentle with those who stir up rebellion against them."

After talking about it far into the night, the neighbors decided that they should get word to the Roman officer. "If we report it in advance, surely the officials will know we had no part in the plot," they assured each other.

The next morning they sought out the officer, and sent word to him that they had knowledge of a plot. The officer came promptly.

"Well?" he said brusquely. "What is it that you would tell me?"

And so the workmen from Nazareth, trembling from fear of the Roman officer and from horror at betraying their neighbor, told about the young Zealot of Nazareth who, having vowed never to work for Rome, had suddenly appeared here at Sepphoris.

The officer had heard of the Zealots. There had been many small outbreaks here and there over the country which they had led. Among those recruited to work on the new city there were men from many towns. It was not possible to know all about each of them. There might be Zealots among them. They might ruin the great buildings that were almost finished. The officer in charge would be held responsible. He would be punished if trouble arose. An uprising here might inflame the whole country. There was not a minute to lose.

Orders were issued quickly. The officer and soldiers began rounding up the workmen. During the next few hours horror followed fast upon horror.

Soon reports began to trickle into Nazareth. The people spoke in whispers. It was too terrible to believe, but it was true. The Romans had captured two thousand men whom they accused of being revolutionists and had put them to death. Many workmen from Nazareth, whose only crime was being in the city, were slain along with the Zealots. The town was filled with sorrowing mothers and fathers and wives and children. But none dared mourn in public.

When Jesus heard the news, deep sadness filled his heart. He grieved especially for his friend, Simon. "There is a better way to save Israel than the way of the sword," he said over and over to himself. Then he prayed, "Show me thy way, O God. Show me thy way."

CHAPTER V

The Wilderness

THE REPORT of the killing of their fellow-townsmen at Sepphoris sobered the young men of Nazareth who had been thinking of joining the Zealots. With the terrible news fresh in the minds of all the people, Jesus hoped they would see that taking the sword against Roman soldiers would only bring upon them more and more suffering. He hoped they would now turn to God and try to learn his way for saving Israel.

Indeed, it seemed for a time as if this was what they would do. The synagogue was crowded, not only on the Sabbath for regular meetings, but for special meetings during the week. The old rabbi was asked many questions. But most of all the people asked, "When will God restore the throne of King David to us, and drive the Romans from our Holy City? When will the Messiah come to save us?"

One evening, after he had finished his work, Jesus went to see the old rabbi. They talked far into the night. From a cabinet on the east wall of his house, the rabbi took the precious scroll of the prophets. Unrolling it carefully, he read the stirring words. "Seek the Lord and ye shall live." "Say to them that are of a fearful heart, 'Be strong, fear not: behold, your God will come and save you.'" "The Lord is a God of judgment: blessed are they that wait for him." "Cease to do evil; learn to do well, seek judgment, relieve the oppressed, judge the fatherless, plead for the widow. If ye be willing and obedient, ye shall eat the good of the land."

Replacing the scroll, the old rabbi sighed. "If only Elijah or Isaiah or Jeremiah would appear among us today. We need a great prophet to stir us. Our people's minds are dull, our hearts are cold. We are poor from Roman taxes and galled by Roman soldiers. It is only our pride that moves us, our pride in our past, in the great kingdom of David."

"And the longing for the Messiah is a longing for a greater David, a mightier conqueror," Jesus added.

There was silence for a moment, as the old rabbi and the young carpenter thought of Israel, their beloved country. Jesus spoke again. "Suppose the people are wrong, Rabbi. Suppose God has another plan. Suppose the Messiah should come to lead the people not in triumph over enemies, but in ways of peace and righteousness. Suppose—"

The old man shook his head. "That is in God's hands. The Messiah will come in God's own time, and will do the work God has appointed him to do."

"You are right, Rabbi," Jesus said as he stood up. "And now I must leave you. It is late and you need your rest."

"And you, my son, need your rest. You are working hard, these days." The old man's face grew tender. "I hear good reports of you. The people of Nazareth say that not even Joseph was a better workman."

The young man flushed. "Thank you, Rabbi. James and Joses are learning rapidly. They can now be depended upon."

"Good. You need help in the carpenter shop. And now, good night. May the Lord bless you and keep you, and your mother, Mary, and all your household."

"The Lord bless you and keep you, Rabbi," Jesus responded

46

gravely. And he started through the night toward his home, knowing he must be at his bench early in the morning.

Though the next day in the carpenter shop proved to be a busy one and James and Joses were both away working on a house, Jesus did not act as if he were in a hurry. He was interested in the people who brought him work as well as in the work, and he liked to talk with them.

When a shepherd came to have his crook mended, Jesus listened eagerly as he worked to what the shepherd told him about the number of new lambs in the flock. When a mother came to order a chest for a daughter engaged to be married, he was happy as he heard about the wedding, and took delight in planning a beautiful chest for the new home.

When someone told him a neighbor was sick and in need of food, he asked Mary to share their bread and cheese.

When a boy came tightly holding a box which had been broken and from which three gray doves were about to escape, he showed the boy how to quiet the frightened doves while he deftly mended the broken box. And when other children came to the door, and asked if they might play with the shavings from his plane, Jesus showed them how to make playthings from the curling wooden ribbons. After they had gone outside, he stood for a moment watching them imitate the piping and singing and dancing they had seen at a village wedding a few weeks before. And when they grew tired and were beginning to quarrel, he put aside his work and called them to come sit on his doorstep and rest a few moments while he told them a story.

Back at his bench, feeling rested, and smiling over the remembered play of his young neighbors, he greeted a farmer who came by to pick up a handle for his scythe, and listened with interest to the news he brought of the crops.

Thus one busy day followed another. Jesus came to be

loved as a good neighbor and trusted as a good workman.

One day, just as he was ready to go to his midday meal, a neighbor stopped at the carpenter shop. "Come, join us at the table," Jesus invited. "Mother brought some fish from the market this morning, and just now I saw her take fresh loaves from the oven yonder." He nodded toward the outdoor brick oven from which came the smoke mingled with the fragrant odor of the morning's baking. Sniffing the air with pleasure, the neighbor accepted the invitation.

After the blessing had been spoken, Mary and the young girls served as Jesus and the neighbor and James and Joses made themselves comfortable about the table, ate their food and talked.

The neighbor had some news. "Have you heard about the journey Ezra, the mason, has taken?"

"Tell us about it," Jesus responded courteously.

"He has gone to the wilderness beyond Jordan."

"Why, what could have taken him on such a journey at this season?" James asked.

The neighbor was pleased that he had news which they had not heard. "It seems that a new prophet is there who is drawing great crowds. A prophet who lives in the wilderness, and wears clothes made of camel's hide and eats only what he finds in the brush and the rocks."

"A queer-sounding prophet," Joses laughed. "Why would anyone go so far to see a man like that?"

The neighbor was annoyed. "They do not go to see him; they go to hear him."

Jesus leaned forward. "Did you say the man is a prophet? What is his message?"

"A message that is stranger than his clothes," the neighbor replied. "Ezra says the prophet talks not of restoring the kingdom of David. Rather, he talks always of the Kingdom of

God." Thoughtfully, almost as if he hesitated to say it, the speaker went on. "The prophet says that the Kingdom of God is at hand. That God's Reign will soon begin."

Joses seemed puzzled. "What does he mean?"

The neighbor shook his head. "Ezra seemed not to be sure. I think that is why he has gone to hear the man."

Jesus was lost in thought. "The Kingdom of God," he mused. "The Reign of God. Men living as God plans, not as kings and rulers and soldiers plan." He felt a growing excitement as his eyes searched the face of his neighbor.

"Does the prophet tell men what they should do to prepare for the coming of the Reign of God?"

"Yes, he does. He says nothing of gathering arms or fighting. He says only that men should repent of their sins and mend their ways to get ready for the Kingdom of God."

James looked slightly shocked. "Repent? Why, then, he must be preaching to Gentiles and sinners. Why does an Israelite like Ezra, who knows the Law, run after him?"

But the neighbor gave little heed to the interruption. "He says we all stand in need of God's forgiveness, even the Pharisees and scribes. Being an Israelite and knowing the Law will not save us. 'Repent and be baptized, cease to do evil, learn to do good, for God's Reign is at hand,' he says over and over."

Jesus was remembering the words of the old rabbi: "If only Elijah or Isaiah or Jeremiah was among us today!" Perhaps God had sent a new prophet to Israel. Perhaps this strange man in the desert would show men the way Israel could be saved.

His food was forgotten now. Jesus was thinking only of the prophet. He must see him. He must hear him. Now. Nothing had ever seemed so important to him.

"What is the man's name?" he asked.

"He is called John the Baptizer."

Jesus rose from the table. "I am going to the wilderness beyond Jordan," he said quietly.

Mary gasped. "But it is so far, Son. Can you leave the shop for so long?"

Her son went to her, touching her gently. "James and Joses are good workmen now. They can manage the shop." He kissed his mother. "The Lord bless you and keep you," he said. He repeated the blessing to the men at the table who were looking up at him in amazement. Then he picked up his cloak and outdoor head covering, and was gone.

"Well! I surely did not expect my news to be so startling," the neighbor said when he had somewhat recovered.

"Nor I, that I should suddenly find myself with a shop to manage," James grumbled.

Joses seemed dazed by the sudden departure. "What could have happened to him?"

At a sound they turned to the corner where Mary sat weeping. "He will never come back," she said. "It was in his face. This strange prophet will take him from me." Gradually she became quiet. She bowed her head. "It is the will of God. For a long time I have known that one day he would go."

While those in the little house in Nazareth were puzzling over his leaving, Jesus was striding through the town. There was no hesitation in his movements. He was on his way to meet this strange new prophet. Perhaps the questions which had been so long in his mind were to be answered. Perhaps the prophet would stir Israel as had the prophets of old.

Scarcely taking time to eat or to sleep along the way, he pushed on. His sandals and his mantle were covered with dust. The keffieh over his head to protect him from the sun was filled with sand. He brushed the insects away with his hand absent-mindedly. Nothing mattered except that he was covering the ground that separated him from the prophet.

He crossed over the ford of the river Jordan. The country grew rough. There were no roads. Yet he met crowds of people going in the same direction. Some were roughly clad, from the countryside of Galilee and from the hills of Judaea. And some were dressed as important city folk dress, in linen tunics and finely woven coats of many colors. The neighbor had been right. The people were going out from the cities and the towns and villages to hear the new prophet.

Suddenly they stopped and listened. They heard the voice, strong and stern, ringing through the wilderness. "Repent! Mend your ways! The Kingdom of God is at hand!"

Jesus went around the crowd and came to a high rock. From this spot he could see the prophet and the people gathered about him, the river flowing back of him, and the rocks and scrubby bushes of the wilderness stretching out on both sides. But his thoughts were not on the surroundings. They were not even on the prophet himself, the strange man clothed in camel's hide. His thoughts were on what the prophet was saying. "God will forgive those who truly repent and mend their ways. Prove that you have repented by ceasing to do evil and doing what is good. For it is with men as with trees. Good trees bring forth good fruit. But if a tree does not bring forth fruit it is cut down and destroyed. So shall it be with you. Repent! Mend your ways! For the Kingdom of God is at hand!"

Now there had come out from Jerusalem certain prominent men of the Pharisees, men who had heard of this strange preacher and wanted to know what he was saying that attracted such crowds. When they had seen the man, they had laughed among themselves. "He is an ignorant man," they had said, "and one who does not keep the Law. See, he does not even wear a tasseled garment to show he is an Israelite."

But as they heard John speak, they felt uneasy. His words stung them. Then, to cover their uneasiness, they spoke haughtily. "We who are the sons of Abraham, Israelites, are the chosen people of God. Why call us to repentance?"

John thundered at them. "Say not, we have Abraham for our father." He swept his hand out toward the mass of brown rocks about them. "I tell you God can raise up from these very stones children to Abraham. But if you would be ready for the Kingdom of God, repent and mend your ways."

The prominent citizens drew their cloaks about them and walked away in disdain.

But the crowds pressed closer. Men began confessing their sins and asking God to forgive them. They came to John to be baptized. "Are you ready to mend your ways?" he asked.

"What must we do? Tell us, and we will do it."

"If you have two coats, share with him who has none. If you have food, do likewise."

A publican came and asked, "What must I do?"

And John said to him, "Do not cheat. Take only the amount of the tax fixed by law."

A soldier came and asked, "What must I do?"

And John said to him, "Do not accuse any man falsely. Be content with money to meet your needs, and do not oppress others to your own advantage."

The people promised to mend their ways, and one by one John baptized them.

As Jesus listened he knew that John was indeed a prophet, speaking words of truth to Israel. To prepare for the Kingdom of God men would not have to wear armor and learn to use the sword. Rather men would have to learn to be good, to do good to others. For God's Kingdom was to be a kingdom of goodness and righteousness, and only good men would have a place in it.

Jesus made his way through the crowd until he was standing in front of the prophet. The rugged man of the desert

glanced at the face before him, ready to ask the usual questions about repentance and mending one's ways. Then he paused and was silent. His helpers looked at him curiously. Why was he hesitating?

"This man is different from the others," John said to them. "His ways are God's ways."

Jesus spoke quietly. "I would be baptized."

John did not ask the questions he had asked the others. His helpers were surprised by his manner. There was no sternness now, but rather humility, strange in the resolute prophet.

"I am not worthy," they heard him say, as he led Jesus to the river and baptized him.

In that moment Jesus knew what God wanted him to do. He had no doubt about it. He knew. His prayer was answered. God spoke to him plainly. He was sent by God to show men God's way to save them. He was to bring Israel to her true greatness as a people of goodness and righteousness, God's people. This was God's will for him. He was God's Son and he would obey his Father.

He had been standing apart from the crowd, conscious only of God and of himself as God's chosen one. Gradually the scene about him came again to mind. The crowds! The people! Farmers and workmen and shepherds and taxgatherers and soldiers and merchants and the learned ones, Pharisees and scribes. He was to win them all, all of Israel, to do God's will. He was to save them, not from the Romans, but from their own sins, sins which were causing more unhappiness and misery in Israel than the Romans caused. He was to prepare men to enter the Kingdom of God, a kingdom of goodness and righteousness and love. He stood transfixed, filled with joy.

The high moment passed. Questions came to mind. How was he to begin? How could he get the people to listen to him?

Should he stay in the wilderness as John did or go to the cities and villages where the people lived?

As these questions began pressing upon him, Jesus walked away from the crowd. Soon he was alone in the wilderness. He was tired and hungry. Could it all have been a dream, that God had chosen him? He was only a carpenter. He was not a learned man, as the great teachers at the Temple were.

Even as the questions came, he knew they were prompted by Satan, not by God. He pushed them from his mind. God had sent him.

But how was he to win the people? They were slow of heart, as the old rabbi had said. Now, the people loved wonder-workers. They would heed his words if he did wonders before them—if he turned stones into bread, or if he should throw himself from a high pinnacle and not be hurt. Yes, the people would flock to hear him if he performed such wonders.

The thought scarcely came before he turned from it. God did not want him to be merely a wonder-worker, amazing the gaping crowds.

But could he become the mighty leader of the nation, one who would have power to say to this one, "Go," and to that one, "Come"? Could he control men and force them to do God's will?

Again the thought repelled him. Wonder-worker, ruler— no, it was not thus that God intended for him to win people.

He fell on his knees. "Show me thy way, O God." And immediately he was comforted. God would show him the way. And whatever the way, he would follow it. He was God's chosen one!

CHAPTER VI

By the Seaside

STANDING alone in the midst of the unfriendly rocks and bushes of the wilderness, Jesus realized that he was very hungry. He had not eaten for days. He smiled to himself. "They tell me that John eats only what he finds in the wilderness," he thought. "Now, let me see if I can do as well as he does about finding food in a barren place."

By-and-by he found some shrubs covered with berries, and in a crevice of a rock some wild honey. Thus he stayed his hunger.

His thoughts turned again to John the Baptizer and all that he had said. John was right about so many matters. He was right about more matters than the great teachers in the Temple had been, Jesus decided. But he was so stern. And he spoke of God as being so stern. God was the righteous judge, as John had said. He did call men to cease to do evil and learn to do good, as the preacher had told all those who sought to be baptized. But, Jesus thought, God was loving, too. He did not just command men to be good, he helped them. Jesus made up his mind to go to John and talk over these questions.

He was nearing the place where John had been preaching.

But where were the crowds? Instead of the multitudes who had been there before, he saw only bushes and rocks and bees. Had the people grown weary of the demands John made upon them? Had they turned away from him? Where was John himself? Jesus hurried on, and came to the bank of the Jordan where John had baptized him.

A slight movement behind one of the rocks attracted his attention, and Jesus saw a man sitting there, stooped over, as though he was too discouraged even to lift his head. Jesus recognized the man as Andrew, one of John's helpers. At the same moment Andrew, roused by a stone dislodged as Jesus walked, raised his eyes. He knew Jesus as the one of whom John had spoken so warmly to his followers. He rose wearily.

"Has no one told you? Told you about John?"

"No one has told me, Andrew. What is it?"

"Herod Antipas has arrested John and thrown him into prison."

"Thrown him into prison? But John is a prophet. Is a prophet not to be allowed to speak in Israel?"

Andrew spoke bitterly. "Not if he offends King Herod."

"For what cause did Herod arrest him, Andrew?"

"For telling the truth! For saying that Herod was wicked, that he had stolen his brother's wife. For this the puppet king our Roman conquerors set over us wants to silence a prophet."

Jesus stood thinking. Herod Antipas had silenced John! Would he silence any prophet who displeased him? What of his own message? Would he, too, be silenced? Would the rulers placed over the country by pagan Romans deal thus with the prophets of Israel as it pleased them? No! God had sent him to speak to the people of Israel, and he would speak. Yet to stay longer where Herod's soldiers might return seeking John's disciples was not wise. He turned to Andrew.

"I am going back to Galilee, Andrew."

Andrew looked at him. How strong he seemed! And not at all afraid. Andrew remembered what John had said of Jesus. Could it be that he also was a prophet? A mightier prophet, even, than John the Baptizer? Andrew wanted to know him better.

"May I go with you?" he asked. "I, too, am from Galilee."

"Come, let us be going."

Leaving the wilderness region, Jesus and Andrew crossed the ford of the Jordan and turned north. They kept to the open country, eating what they could find, and when night came, sleeping on the ground with only their cloaks for bedding. The next day they came into Galilee. The land had changed, now. Instead of the rocky soil of the wilderness country, they saw fields of wheat and barley, vineyards heavy with growing grapes, orchards of palms and figs, and groves of gray-green olive trees.

"It is good to be back in Galilee," Jesus said.

They stood for a moment, watching a farmer at work with a hoe, trying to get rid of some thistles growing in the midst of his grain. When the farmer saw the travelers, he called to them to rest a while and share his bread and cheese.

As they sat talking after their meal, Jesus asked the farmer about his crops. "Most of the fields will have a good yield," the man answered. "Some of the soil is better than the rest of it. See, over there the wheat is taller and the heads heavier than on this side of the field."

Andrew remembered the rocky soil of the wilderness. "But all your soil is good compared to that of the wilderness regions beyond Jordan. There any crop would have a hard time growing because of the rocks."

"Yes, God is good to us in Galilee," the farmer agreed. "The fields yield grain to provide us bread, the olive trees provide us oil for our lamps, the fruit trees and vines give us dates and figs and grapes, and the Sea of Galilee provides fish."

Andrew stood up. "The sea provides fish when the fishermen fish," he said. "I am a fisherman. It is time I returned to the nets."

Thanking the farmer for his kindness to passing travelers, Andrew and Jesus went on their way.

"You are a fisherman, Andrew? You live by the sea?"

"Near Capernaum," Andrew answered. "My brother, Peter, and I are partners with James and John, the sons of Zebedee." Then he added, "I have been away some time."

They walked for a while in silence. Andrew was thinking of Jesus. Wondering if he was a great prophet. Wondering if he would stir the people as John the Baptizer had done. He was not like John. He was gentler, more friendly toward the people they passed along the way, more interested in their daily work. He seemed to like people more, to want to be friends with them.

It was growing dark as they came toward Capernaum. There were more people on the road now, going to do business in the city on the Sea of Galilee. The crowds increased as they entered the city. Jesus had not been to Capernaum before, so Andrew took the lead, showing the way through the darkening streets.

"Will you go with me to the boat?" he asked. "There will be a moon tonight. My brother and our partners will be there, ready to go out fishing."

Jesus nodded. "It should be a good night for fishing."

The wind was freshening. It brought to them the strong smell of fish from the sea. Another turn, and they saw the water. The moon was rising, touching the little waves with silver. All along the shore the fishing boats were being made ready for the night's catch. Barefoot men were gathering up their great nets and stowing them aboard. Then wading knee-

deep in the water, they would push their boats off, climb aboard, and hoist their sails into the moonlight. Jesus watched the busy scene about him, his face alive with interest. It was all new to him. How intent the men were upon their work!

He followed Andrew to the edge of the water. They found the fishermen, Peter, James, and John, just ready to push off.

"I'm glad you have come, Andrew," Peter called as he saw his brother on shore. "I need you in the boat."

There was not time to talk, but Peter spoke courteously to his brother's companion. "There is room at my house for you, and you will be welcome there." He beckoned to a neighbor standing near. "Will you direct the stranger to my house?"

When the neighbor agreed readily, Peter turned back to Jesus. "We will greet you in the morning when we return from the sea," he said, and the fishermen pushed their boats into the water.

Early the next morning, Jesus went again to the seashore. People were gathering to watch the boats come in.

One boat landed, its nets heavy with the gleaming motion of a large catch. Quickly the men were at work, sorting the fish, tossing the good ones into baskets for the market, and throwing the bad ones back into the sea.

Another boat landed. This one had only a fair catch, and the men moved with less spirit. They sighed as they made fast their boat, and began sorting their fish. "There will be little profit from this night's work," one of them said to another.

More boats came in, some with a good catch, some with a poor catch.

By-and-by, Jesus saw Peter and Andrew and James and John. They pulled their boats to shore and began struggling with the heavy, dripping nets. The nets were limp. The men had caught nothing. Tired and discouraged, they made ready to mend the nets for the next trip.

Jesus came near and Andrew greeted him warmly. It was difficult for the other fishermen to be courteous to their guest. Andrew had talked about him with enthusiasm as they had started on the night's trip, and they had been interested. But the long, profitless night had left them weary and dispirited. Even if the stranger should be a prophet, as Andrew thought, what could he say to fishermen who had caught no fish? They bent over their nets.

But as Jesus began to talk, they listened. "Be not anxious about the catch," he said. "There are many fish in the sea, and God knows that you need food. But there are men in Israel who are not living as God would have men live. They seek power as the heathen do. God is calling upon them to repent and to turn again to him and learn his ways. For the Kingdom of God is at hand."

The net slipped from Peter's grasp. God's Kingdom at hand! Could this stranger mean that at last God was to save Israel from the Romans? That the Roman taxes and the Roman soldiers would plague Israel no more? He was giving his whole attention to Jesus. The others were leaning forward.

"Come, Andrew. Come, Peter. Come, James and John. Come with me. God has sent me to call men to prepare themselves to be members of God's Kingdom. Come with me, and fish for men."

Andrew looked at his brother. Peter had always been the leader. What was he thinking? Would he believe that Jesus was a prophet? The big fisherman, his face and chest burned deep brown by the sun on the water, the muscles of his strong arms standing out, was trembling.

"But I am a sinful man," he cried.

"Repent and God will forgive your sins, Peter. And you will bring other men to repentance. I tell you, God's Kingdom is at hand."

Gazing intently into the face before him, Peter knew that Jesus was a prophet, sent by God. He knew that he, Peter the fisherman, was chosen by God to share the prophet's work.

Without a word he stood up, motioning to the others to help him. The fishermen drew their boats onto the shore, turned them bottom-side up, and spread the nets to dry.

CHAPTER VII

The Busy Town

THE FOUR sturdy fishermen, their coats still tucked into their girdles where they had caught them up to keep them out of the water, tied their sandals on their feet, and looked at Jesus.

"We will go with you, Teacher," Peter said for them all.

The fishermen had long awaited the day when Israel would be saved. They were stirred when Jesus said that the Kingdom of God was at hand. They thought he was a prophet. They did not wait to learn what he meant by the Kingdom of God. They were willing to go with him because they were drawn to him as a person. They trusted him. And so by the seashore they promised to be his disciples.

It was the day before the Sabbath. Some business had to be cared for and some food bought before sunset, when the three long blasts of the trumpet from the roof of the synagogue would announce the coming of the Sabbath and all work must cease.

While the fishermen were in the city markets, Jesus sat by the sea on the upturned boat, thinking of them. He knew that these, his first disciples, were unlearned men who had worked hard with their hands and who had thought but little of many of the matters which were so important to him. But he knew, too, that they were men who wanted to be good, loyal to their country and obedient to God. And so he accepted them as they were. He saw them returning now and went to meet them.

As the four fishermen walked with Jesus toward Peter's house, they said little, each one busy with his own thoughts. The notes of the synagogue trumpet rang out over the city just as they reached the door.

When the Sabbath lamps were lighted in the house, the men gathered about the table while Peter's wife and his mother-in-law stood ready to serve them. Peter turned to Jesus. "Will you lead the Sabbath prayers, Teacher?"

The old, familiar words took on fresh meaning as Jesus spoke them.

"Remember the Sabbath day to keep it holy. Six days shalt thou labor and do all thy work, but the seventh day is a sabbath unto the Lord thy God.

"Blessed art thou, O Lord our God, King of the universe. Who has hallowed us by thy commandments and in love and favor hast given us thy holy Sabbath.

"Blessed art thou, O Lord our God, who bringest forth bread from the earth. We thank thee, O Lord our God, because thou dost give us an heritage, a good and ample land, the covenant and the Law, and food in plenty."

After the Sabbath meal had been eaten, the men went out-of-doors. The evening breeze from the sea rustled the leaves on the fig tree under which they sat. Peter and Andrew and James and John found many questions in their minds, ordinary questions. Where was the Teacher from? Had he traveled to far places? Had he gone to school to the great teachers? Even as the questions were stirring, Jesus told them that he had lived in Nazareth of Galilee, that he was a workman like themselves, that he had gone to no school except to

the village synagogue, that he had been to Jerusalem, but had been nowhere else outside of his own neighborhood.

The men were surprised, but they were not troubled. They knew little of the great schools and the famous teachers. Often they had said among themselves that the rabbis and scribes and the visiting teachers who came to the synagogue of Capernaum spoke of matters far from the lives of the fishermen. The Pharisees who ruled the synagogue insisted upon many ceremonies about food and washings, and many fasts and special prayers which people who worked long hours found it hard to observe. Perhaps because this Teacher was a workman and not a man of the schools he would be more concerned about things that mattered to an ordinary man. And so the disciples felt content.

They had slept none the night before, and had had little rest during the day. Their eyelids grew heavy. It was time to go to sleep.

On the morning of the Sabbath, Jesus woke early and got up from the pallet spread for him on the flat roof of Peter's house. He looked out over the city of Capernaum, its noises hushed in the quiet of the Sabbath morning; on to the Sea of Galilee, lying blue and peaceful between its sheltering hills; and then on beyond where the sun was touching the snow on Mount Hermon. The peak of this towering mountain he had seen often from the hills of Nazareth. How long ago it seemed since he had been a boy gazing at Hermon! He thought of Nazareth, of the home there, of the carpenter shop where James and Joses now worked at his bench, and of his mother, Mary. He thought of the synagogue where they would soon be going on this Sabbath morning, and of the old rabbi who had taught him so long. He asked God's blessing on them all.

His thoughts came back to Capernaum. It was in this busy city that he would carry on the work God had sent him to do.

The morning meal was ready, and Jesus went down the narrow outside stairway to join the others. The men had on clean white tunics now, their striped coats were carefully brushed, their girdles neatly tied. They were ready to go to the synagogue. Soon they were on their way up the hill, the men walking in front, the women following after.

As they came near the synagogue, Jesus stood to one side a moment, watching the people coming from all directions. The farmer in whose field he and Andrew had eaten was there. He had on a new tunic; his face was satisfied, as if he was thinking of the good crops in his fields. He must not forget God who brings the grain to a head. He had come to the synagogue to pray and to give thanks.

A carpenter was there, weary after a busy week. Jesus knew the marks of his trade. And a shepherd came, fresh out of the hills where he had been tending his flocks, eager for human companionship after his lonely week's work. Some strangers, too, were coming, men whom the Sabbath found on the road, far from their homes. The poor were there, those who had no work to claim their attention during the week, the discouraged, and the friendless. Even some outcasts came, and those who lived by begging and petty thieving. They knew they were despised by the chief men of the synagogue, yet they knew, too, that none dared refuse them admission. The Scriptures read in the synagogue were for all the people of Israel.

Making their way through the gathering crowd came the Pharisees, the important men of the city, their cloaks finely woven, the fringe heavy on their shawls. They looked as if they had had a profitable week in their businesses and were pleased with themselves because they had observed all requirements of the Law. Theirs were the front seats in the synagogue.

As Jesus watched the people entering, he felt a great upsurge of love for them. He knew that many of them, even on the Sabbath as they came to the synagogue to worship God, were thinking, too, of their own affairs. Yet they were his people. He longed to help them to be rid of their fears, their loneliness, their sin, their hypocrisy, their self-satisfaction. He was sure that God wanted him to speak to them. Today. Here. At the synagogue. He would speak for God.

Those who had come with him had been waiting curiously. "Why is Jesus standing so still, watching the people?" Andrew asked his brother.

Peter's face was puzzled. "Why, he looks as if he loves these people," he said. "To me they are not a very lovable lot. And he does not even know them."

James frowned, as if trying to find an answer to a question. "He seems a simple man, Peter, like you and me and Andrew and John, not a learned man like the scribes. Yet he is different, too. How is he different?"

Without answering, Peter wheeled around. "I am going to ask the president of the synagogue to invite Jesus to speak." Before the others could reply, Peter was gone.

Now, it was the custom for the president of the synagogue to ask visiting teachers to read the Scriptures and to speak to the people. When Peter told him of the new Teacher, the president came to Jesus and invited him courteously.

Without a moment's hesitation, Jesus followed the president into the synagogue and took the seat which was offered to him, facing the congregation.

CHAPTER VIII

The Synagogue

THE PEOPLE in the synagogue strained this way and that to see the visitor. "Who is he?" they whispered to one another. "Where is he from?" No one seemed to know anything about the visiting Teacher.

The service was beginning. The people grew still. Then came the familiar words: "Hear, O Israel, the Lord thy God is one God. And thou shalt love the Lord thy God with all thy heart, and with all thy soul, and with all thy strength."

After the prayer, the president parted the curtains at the front of the room and from the ark he reverently took out the scroll which he handed to Jesus. The visitor stood up and, when he had found the place, he began to read the passage which the people of Israel had heard so often. But as Jesus read the words they seemed to come alive as they had never done before. "The spirit of the Lord is upon me because he hath sent me to preach the good news to the poor; he hath sent me to heal the broken-hearted, to preach deliverance to captives, and recovering of sight to the blind, to set at liberty them that are bruised; to preach the acceptable year of the Lord." When he had finished reading, Jesus returned the scroll to the president, and sat down, as the custom was, to speak to the people.

"People of Capernaum, give heed to the word of God which has been read in your hearing," he began. He looked toward the self-satisfied ones. He must make them think of God's way for them. "God's Kingdom will soon come! Prepare yourselves for it. Think of God and his love and righteousness, and his way for you. Care for those who need your help and be generous in your dealings with all men. If you follow God's way, you and your country will be saved."

As his eyes fell upon the lonely ones huddled together at the back of the synagogue, his voice softened. "God knows you have need of food and clothes and shelter. He cares even for the birds of the air; yet you are far more precious to him than these are. Repent of your sins, and have faith in God. He cares for you."

The men in the front places looked at one another with raised eyebrows. "Who is this man?" they seemed to be asking. "He presumes to speak very positively. Yet we have never heard of him. And what does he mean by saying the Kingdom of God will soon come?"

Those who were in the back of the synagogue heard him in wonder. Did he mean that God cared for them, even for them? That it mattered to God whether they were hungry or cold or miserable? That it mattered even whether they stole or lied?

In the gallery behind the lattice where they sat, the women, too, were listening. They were weary of the endless drawing of water for the washing of hands in accordance with the rules laid down by the scribes. They were weary of the extra work required in the preparation of the bread, and in the dressing of the meat so that it might be declared clean according to the Law. Did the Teacher mean that they were important to God?

Suddenly the quiet of the synagogue was shattered. A

shrill voice cried out, "Jesus of Nazareth, why are you here? What have you to do with us? We know who you are. You are a prophet of God."

The people all knew who had cried out. It was a man of Capernaum who had strange attacks. It was said he was possessed of a demon, an evil spirit. The children were afraid of him, often the young men made fun of him, and the men and women shunned him.

The men on the front seats of the synagogue were clearly disgusted. It was unseemly that the service should be interrupted. The man should be put out. He should be chained so that he could not go about disturbing decent people.

But Jesus studied the man's face with compassion. He understood what was needed. He spoke firmly but gently. "Be quiet. You will be tormented by evil spirits no more."

For so long the man had received only looks of fear or loathing. Now he saw kindness in a face. Someone cared about him! The man fell down with a loud cry.

"Has the demon come out of him?" the people were whispering excitedly. They watched in amazement as the man stood up, his eyes fastened upon Jesus. Why, the man was in his right mind! The wildness had gone out of him. He stood as other men stood; his face had become as other men's faces.

The president hastily spoke the final blessing and the people began leaving the synagogue. Outside they crowded around the man whom they had known for so long as one out of his mind. They stared at him. They asked him questions. There could be no doubt about it. The man was now able to think and to talk as other men did.

"What is this?" they said to one another. "Is this a new prophet with power over evil? Who does wonderful deeds of healing?"

The people scattered and went to their own homes. But all

over Capernaum the word went out that there was a new prophet in the city. That he spoke with authority. That he had power over evil spirits which they thought caused all illness.

"Maybe he can cure my child," a mother said as she stood anxiously over the pallet where a sick child lay.

"Maybe he can make me well," a boy said who had long felt weak and miserable.

"Maybe he will save me from the evil spirits which torment me," another man said.

That afternoon people all over the city were talking about the new prophet. They learned that he was staying in the house of Peter, the fisherman. As soon as the sun had set and the Sabbath was ended, they started toward Peter's door.

Peter and Andrew and James and John had been pleased when they saw how the people at the synagogue had listened to Jesus. They had been amazed when the man they had known so long as out of his mind had spoken clearly and looked at them with eyes that were quiet.

"He is a greater prophet than John the Baptizer," Andrew said.

"So it would seem," Peter agreed.

"And we are his first disciples," James exclaimed proudly.

Jesus heard the words they were saying, and came to them. "Did you not understand? Only one thing is important: that men know God's way for them."

But James was not listening. He was remembering the people. "Teacher, the people are telling the whole city about you. They know you are a great prophet. Why, right now you are the most famous man in Capernaum."

Even as James spoke, Peter saw the people coming. "Look!" he cried, "they are seeking you out. The whole city is here!"

James ran to the door. "Even some of the Pharisees are

coming," he reported. John hurried after him. "See, there is Isaac," he called excitedly. "He has the biggest market in Capernaum."

Jesus followed the others to the door. He saw the sick ones and the unhappy ones and the lonely ones. He paid no attention to those who had come out of curiosity and who were now standing apart on the outskirts of the crowd. His thoughts were all for those who needed comfort and love and help. He felt within himself the power of God, given to him to help people. And so he stepped out of the doorway and moved among the crowd.

He took the sick child from his mother's arms and smiled into the pinched face and touched the hot forehead. Then he gave the child back to his mother. "He will be well," he said confidently. And the mother knew the child was better!

He took the hand of the boy who had felt weak and miserable for so long, and looked into his eyes. "You will feel stronger now," he said. "Do not worry about yourself. God cares for you."

He called to the man who had been tormented by evil spirits, and told him to trust God and not to fear the evil spirits.

From one to the other he went, speaking comforting words, soothing aching foreheads, talking always of God's love for men, urging them to trust God and not be afraid. It grew dark, but the people continued to come, and Jesus continued to minister to them.

It was far into the night before the last one had gone. Jesus had helped all those who needed help. He was tired. He turned to his disciples. "The Lord bless you and keep you," he said as his good night to them, and went up the narrow stairs to the pallet on the roof.

For a long time he sat quietly. He thought of all that had

happened during the busy day. He had begun the work God had sent him to do. The people had heard him gladly. Yet they were more eager to see wonders than they were to hear of God's way of righteousness for them. Because he loved people, he wanted to help the sick to be well. But he was not sent to be merely a wonder-worker. He was sent to teach men to follow God's ways so that they and their country might be saved. He prayed to God to show him what to do on the morrow. Then he went to sleep.

It was scarcely light the next morning when the first people came to Peter's door. Soon a crowd was pressing about the house.

Peter woke up and ran to the door. "Why, there is a larger crowd than there was yesterday," he called to the others. "I must wake the Teacher." As he hurried away, John and James were talking.

"The people of Capernaum have never gone out to any other man as they are coming to Jesus," James said. "Why, it may mean—"

He stopped as Peter ran in, his face surprised and angry. "He isn't there!" he almost shouted.

"Not there? What do you mean?"

"His pallet is folded up, and he has gone away. That is what I mean," Peter said irritably.

"But where could he have gone?"

"Why did he leave?"

"What shall we tell the people?"

"How can we find him and bring him back?"

The questions flew back and forth, as the four disciples stood not knowing what to think or what to do.

"I will go look for him," Peter decided. "He can't have gone far. Maybe he wanted to get away from the crowds for a little while."

Peter hurried through the streets to the place by the sea where they had talked with Jesus the day before the Sabbath. But he was not there. "He may have gone out toward the hills," he thought finally. "I remember he said he liked to climb the hills in Nazareth." So Peter trudged up the hillside beyond the synagogue. And there he found Jesus, sitting on a high rock, his face serene, as though he had been praying.

He saw Peter, hot and panting from his hurried climb. "Come, sit here with me and rest awhile, Peter." The angry words that had been on Peter's lips died. But he did not sit down. He stood, puzzled and hurt and annoyed.

"Why did you leave, Teacher?" he asked. "There is a great crowd by our door. The whole city is seeking you. Come, let us hurry back before the people grow weary and leave."

But Jesus shook his head. "No, Peter. Rather let us go now to the other towns and cities."

"But Capernaum is an important city!" Peter cried out. "There are important people here, and you can find many followers. They want to hear you."

Jesus spoke calmly. "Rather they want to see wonders, Peter. Let us go to the other towns and cities for a while. Then we will come back. I was not sent to be a wonder-worker."

Peter did not understand. He wanted the Teacher to return to the crowds. But he knew that Jesus would do only what he thought was right. With a sigh, Peter turned.

"Wait here and I will bring the others," he said, and strode off down the hill.

CHAPTER IX

Throughout Galilee

As Peter led Andrew and James and John to the hill where he had left Jesus, they were all full of disappointment.

"He wanted to tell men about the Kingdom of God," James grumbled. "Why doesn't he stay where men are? Men who are ready to listen to him?"

"But what did he say, Peter?" John kept asking. "Why did he say he went away?"

"I tell you I know no more about it than you do," Peter retorted impatiently. "He said we would go to the other places, because he was sent to minister to men who needed him."

"Well, aren't there people in Capernaum who need him?" James demanded.

John kicked a rock savagely. "I hope he hasn't thrown away his best opportunity," he muttered.

Andrew spoke as if thinking out loud. "There are people here who need him, yes, and people who listen to what he says to them. But there are so many people in a busy city who would flock around any new teacher, especially if they heard he was doing wonders. The idle. The curious. Perhaps he thinks it would be better to go for a while to the little villages and the towns."

"There he is." The others scanned the hillside toward which Peter pointed. Jesus was sitting just as Peter had left him. But when he saw his four disciples he came to meet them. "I am glad you came," he said simply. The four men standing before him, a little sullen, a little ashamed of themselves, gazed at him searchingly. They did not know why they had come. They had not wanted to come. They thought he had made a mistake to leave the city just as people were learning of him. But they had never known anyone like him. He had won their hearts.

Again, Peter spoke for them all. "We will go with you, Teacher."

Walking toward the highway, they passed the synagogue and stopped on the wide steps of the porch to look for a moment at the city and the Sea of Galilee.

They found they were not alone. Across the broad porch just inside the door, a man was standing with his head bowed, saying humbly over and over, "God be merciful to me, a sinner; God be merciful to me, a sinner."

"Why, isn't that Matthew, the publican?" Peter asked, and stepped closer to the door. He turned and nodded.

James' lips curled scornfully. "And well may a tax collector for the Romans ask God's mercy."

Another voice came to them from inside the synagogue, this one strong and confident. Startled, they looked through the door and saw Isaac, the Pharisee, praying aloud. "God, I thank thee that I am not as other men are, cheaters, unjust, adulterers. Or even as this publican behind me. I fast twice in each week; I give tithes of all I possess. Prosper, O God, my family and my buying and selling."

As the haughty voice ceased speaking, Jesus led the disciples down the steps and onto the road.

"Isaac was in the crowd which came to hear you yesterday,"

79

Peter remarked. Then he added, "He is a very important man in Capernaum."

"And a very proud man, Peter," Jesus replied. "I tell you that the prayer of the publican standing in the doorway was more pleasing to God than the prayer of the Pharisee in the chief place."

The faces of the disciples showed surprise. James whispered to John, "How can a publican's prayer ever be pleasing to God?" But none of them questioned the Teacher aloud.

During the next few weeks the four fishermen began to learn what Jesus had meant when he asked them to come with him and fish for men. From one village of Galilee to another they went, stopping to talk with farmers as they swung their scythes through the fields of ripe grain, and with vinedressers as they mended the walls of their vineyards, and with merchants in their booths, and with carpenters as they smoothed wood in their shops.

Whenever they passed a crippled person along the way, Jesus took time to help him. Whenever they met a little child, he paused for a merry greeting. And even to the dirty wayside beggars from whom most men shrank away, he spoke kindly.

One day as they were passing through a hilly section of the country, they saw a shepherd searching here and there. Jesus spoke to him. "Have you lost a sheep?"

"Yes, a baby lamb has wandered away."

"We will help you," Jesus promised, and before the disciples realized what had happened, they were peering under bushes and among rocks seeking to find a baby lamb. As darkness was falling the shepherd called over the ravine, "I have found the lamb!" And what rejoicing there was!

Another day they saw people tormenting a dumb man. Bewildered and afraid, the man was making strange sounds. "A devil has taken him," someone called out. But Jesus knew

the man need not be dumb. He spoke to him, and the dumb man looked into eyes that were kind. He was not afraid any more. Instead of the strange mumblings, the people standing around heard clear words.

"The man can speak!" they exclaimed to one another. And the news soon spread through the village.

On yet another day Jesus and the disciples were near the market place of a town when they saw a Roman officer stride haughtily toward a group of men in the market square. "You," he called out to a young man. "You are idle. Come, carry a pack for me." He smiled an evil smile. "It is only a mile that you must go."

The young man's face turned pale. He knew the officer had the right under the law to demand this service. But a proud son of Abraham would not be forced to be servant to a Roman soldier!

Jesus saw what was about to happen. The young man would resist. He might be killed. Certainly he would be arrested and might spend the rest of his life in prison. Jesus, too, resented the order from a foreign soldier. But it was not worth while to lose a man's life over carrying a pack.

He stepped up to the officer and offered pleasantly, "I will carry the pack for you." Then he smiled as if he had thought of a secret bit of fun. "In fact, I will carry it *two* miles instead of the one you may require under the law."

In all the months he had been in Israel, the officer had never heard such a reply. He stood gaping. The people in the market square laughed at his discomfiture as Jesus hoisted the pack to his shoulder and swung off down the road.

"Why did the Teacher do it?" a bystander asked the disciples.

James was scowling. "I don't know. I wish he hadn't. I would not have done it."

"Neither would I," Peter said, his eyes on the Roman officer. Then he chuckled. "Have you ever seen a haughty Roman so taken aback? He looks almost as if he is ashamed!"

Andrew answered the bystander more directly. "It seems that Jesus chose the best way to deal with the Roman."

So the days were spent, going from village to village, finding people who needed help and ministering to them. On the Sabbath they would go to the synagogue in whatever town they were, and often Jesus was asked to teach.

In one place after another, people began to tell their friends about the new Teacher. "He speaks so we can understand him," they said. "And he helps people along the way who have no claim upon him."

Soon, wherever he went, people gathered about him, and he taught them. Sometimes it was a small group; sometimes a large crowd. All sorts of people came: good and bad, sick and well, rich and poor, men of Israel and men from foreign lands, the Pharisees who observed all the ceremonies and laws, and the outcasts who observed few of them. He turned no one away, but spoke to them all as if he was interested in each one and thought each one was a person important to God.

Always Jesus spoke of the love of God for men and of the need for all men to turn to God and follow his way, the way of righteousness and love.

"Become again as a little child," he would say, "and trust in God as your father. Let God make you over so you will want only what God wants. God will show you what to do. And both you and Israel will be saved."

Often he drew pictures in words to show them what he wanted them to understand.

"If you turn to God and follow his way, then will you be wise, as a man was who built his house on a rock. The storms came and the rains descended and the winds blew upon the house, but it stood firm, for it was built upon a rock. But if you do not turn to God and mend your ways, then you will be like a man who built his house upon the sand. The storms came and the rain descended and the winds blew upon the house, and it fell and was broken into pieces, because it was built upon the sand."

When Jesus saw people who were tired and discouraged and worn out with work too heavy for them to do, he would speak lovingly to them. "Come, you who are weary and have burdens too heavy to bear. Come. Tell me of your burdens. To share them will give you rest. It will be as if we were under a yoke together, you and I, bearing the burden together." And the people heard him gladly.

The crowds grew greater. "He is a prophet, sent by God," the people said as they thronged about him, listening to his words, and bringing their sick to him.

The four disciples marveled at his words of wisdom and his wonderful deeds of mercy.

"There was never so great a prophet," Andrew said to the others one evening.

"Never, Andrew, not in all Israel," Peter agreed. "And yet he chose men like us to be his disciples!"

James smiled with satisfaction. "Great honor should come to us."

"When the Kingdom is set up we should have important places," John added.

One Sabbath afternoon in early summer, the disciples were going with Jesus from one village to the next one. They had had no food all day and were hungry. Passing through a field, the disciples took some ripe grain from the stalks, rubbed it between their hands and ate it. Now, the Law forbade the gathering and threshing of grain on the Sabbath. Some Pharisees who saw what the disciples had done were offended.

They met Jesus as he came out of the field. "Why do your disciples do that which is not lawful on the Sabbath?" they demanded. "Do they not know the Law forbids men to harvest grain on the Sabbath?"

The disciples became uneasy, for they did not wish to offend the Pharisees. But Jesus answered the men directly.

"The Law does forbid men to harvest grain on the Sabbath. But when men are hungry, is it not right to meet their need on the Sabbath? Is plucking a few grains and rubbing off the husks in a man's hand the same as cutting and threshing a harvest? I tell you, no. God made the Sabbath to help men, not to lay burdens upon men."

The answer did not satisfy the questioners. "The Law is the Law," they said to one another as they walked away. "Whether a man harvests grain with his hand to stay his hunger or reaps it with a scythe to take to market, he is guilty of breaking the Law."

In the next village they reported to the president of the synagogue what had happened.

Thus it came about that on the Sabbath, when Jesus and his disciples went to the synagogue as was their custom, the president did not wish to ask Jesus to speak. But many people were there who had heard about him from friends in other villages.

"We would hear this Teacher in our synagogue," they insisted, and the president was persuaded to invite him.

As he began to speak, Jesus looked toward the women's gallery. He saw there a woman who seemed to be suffering. Her face was twisted with pain and mental torment, and her body was bent. Her misery called out to him for help. Jesus stopped speaking. "Woman," he said gently, "you need no longer be in pain and misery. You are free of your torment."

The woman did not know what had happened. But she

did know that whereas she had been bowed down with wretchedness, now she could stand erect; that whereas her mind had been black with fear, now it was clear. She spoke out in her joy. "Praise be to God! Praise be to God!"

But the president of the synagogue was angry. He bustled about seeking to quiet the people. "Do you not know that this is the Sabbath?" he demanded. "There are six days during which work can be done. Come during the week and be healed, but not on the Sabbath."

The Pharisees, the leading citizens who occupied the front seats, nodded their heads. One of them spoke to Jesus. "Do you pretend to be a teacher, yet do not keep the Law? We tell you again, it is not lawful to work on the Sabbath."

Jesus spoke to them sharply. "I do not break God's Law of the Sabbath, but keep it. Do not each one of you loose your oxen or your cattle and lead them to water on the Sabbath that they may drink? That, you say, is permitted. Yet would you say it is against God's Law to free a woman, a daughter of Abraham, from her misery?"

The president of the synagogue was silenced, but some of the Pharisees still insisted that Jesus had broken the Law.

"He has also taught others to treat the Law lightly," one of them added, frowning as he saw the people gathering around the woman.

"His teaching is dangerous," another Pharisee said. And they went away angry.

But the people rejoiced over the good deed Jesus had done among them. And his fame spread throughout Galilee.

CHAPTER X

The Publican's House

Jesus and his disciples had completed a circuit of Galilee, and now they were again near Capernaum. Peter was wondering about the people who had been clamoring to see Jesus when they left the city. Would they have forgotten him? Or would they come again? He understood a little better now why Jesus had wanted to leave when he did, but he still was puzzled about it.

As the travelers came into the city, they passed the tax-gatherer's office. Matthew was there, counting his money. The four disciples turned their faces away. A passing youth jeered, "See the publican counting his money! A man of Israel collecting taxes for the Romans!"

Jesus stepped nearer. His shadow fell over the money. Matthew did not glance up. He was accustomed to scorn. "What is it?" he asked mechanically.

Jesus spoke his name. "Matthew."

Why, the voice was friendly! Matthew looked up. As he recognized Jesus he stared wonderingly. He had been outside listening the morning Jesus had spoken in the Capernaum synagogue. Later he had been on the fringes of the crowd that had gathered about Peter's door. He had seen how Jesus had healed and comforted and cheered the people who came to him. He had longed to go to him himself. But he had not had the courage. He had gone instead to the synagogue alone to ask God's forgiveness.

Now Jesus was here. At this despised place, the office of the tax collector for the Romans.

The disciples were standing by, rooted in their steps. What! Was Jesus stopping at the tax collector's office? Was he speaking to Matthew, the publican?

When they heard his next words they could hardly believe their ears. For Jesus was saying, "Come, Matthew. Leave your taxgathering and be my disciple."

Matthew could not believe it, either. For so long he had had no friends. The only persons in all the city to whom he could speak without risking scorn were the other tax collectors. And now this Teacher was asking him to go with him. Someone trusted him!

Matthew scarcely glanced at the money as he turned it over to his assistant. "I shall not be back," he said, and hurried out to join Jesus.

Peter and Andrew and James and John walked behind. A despised publican in their group! Why had the Teacher done it? They asked the question over and over as they followed Jesus and Matthew through the streets of Capernaum.

"One thing is sure," Peter said. "There will be no crowds around my door waiting for him now. Not even the common people will come to him. And as for the Pharisees—" He ended with a gesture of discouragement.

James finished the statement. "They would think they were unclean forever if they came near a publican."

John nodded. "Try to imagine Isaac, the merchant, in the same group with Matthew, the publican."

But Andrew was remembering. "John the Baptizer received publicans who repented. He told them to repent and mend their ways just as he told all the others to repent. Even the Pharisees. And then he baptized the publicans as he did everyone else who repented."

"How can publicans repent?" Peter wanted to know. "Their work is evil. They are traitors to their country every time they collect tax money for our conquerors."

James was angry. "Besides, they cheat the people. They take more than they should. Why, they would have to stop being publicans if they repented."

"That is not what John said," Andrew insisted. "He told them only that they would have to stop cheating people. I remember what he said. 'Never take more than the rate fixed by the law.'"

James turned on him. "Do you mean that a man can work for our enemies, the Romans, and at the same time be preparing himself for the Kingdom of God? Bah!"

John agreed. "Do not talk foolishness, Andrew. A man cannot be a good Israelite and collect money for our conquerors to hire soldiers to rule over us."

But Andrew reminded the others of what Matthew had said as he left his office. "Matthew is not going to be a tax collector any longer. We heard him tell his assistant that he would not be back."

Peter motioned toward Matthew, deep in conversation with Jesus. "Look! Why, Matthew seems like a different man."

"The hard, greedy expression is gone," Andrew added wonderingly.

"What does it mean?" Peter asked. There was something like awe in his voice. "Can it mean that Jesus has caused a publican to repent? That Matthew has been forgiven?"

So concerned had the disciples been about the publican

that they had followed after Jesus and Matthew scarcely noticing where they were going. Now James stopped. "See where we are going. We are going to Matthew's house!"

John was dismayed. "Jesus is at the door. Will he enter a publican's house?"

While John spoke, Matthew went inside, but Jesus waited at the door.

As the unhappy disciples came up to him, Jesus spoke to them gently. "Do you not understand? It is not God's purpose that one of his children should be turned away from him. He loves each one of them, publicans, foreigners, Pharisees, fishermen, farmers, housewives, little children. If any one repents and turns to God, God will welcome him into his Kingdom."

Peter felt again just as he had felt when Jesus went away from Capernaum and left the eager crowds before his door. He felt baffled, bewildered. "What would you have us do, Teacher?" he asked.

The answer came direct and clear. "Accept Matthew as one of you. Trust him. Be friends with him. He will be a faithful and useful helper."

Even as the four men were trying to overcome their prejudices against Matthew, the publican, Jesus called upon them to do more.

"Matthew is giving a dinner for me this evening."

The disciples gasped. "You would not have us eat with a publican, Teacher?" James cried out sharply.

"Who would come to a dinner in the home of a tax collector?" Peter demanded.

Jesus smiled. "Not the Pharisees, certainly, Peter." He knew he was asking something which it would be hard even for the men who loved him to do. Yet they must understand that he was sent to help all men.

"No, none of the respectable people of Capernaum will come. But the other tax collectors will come. They are the ones Matthew is going to invite."

Jesus wanted to give the disciples a little time to think about it all before they decided whether to come to the dinner or not. "There is yet an hour before time for dinner," he told them. "I will go in and rest awhile," and he entered Matthew's house.

The four disciples talked for the entire hour about what Jesus had asked them to do.

"I do not understand why he asks us to do it," Peter said finally, "but because I love him, I cannot turn my back on him." And the others agreed.

Thus it came about that Jesus and Peter and Andrew and James and John ate dinner in the home of a publican, surrounded at the table by other publicans.

The tax collectors, for their part, had been as amazed by the invitation as the disciples had been. When Matthew had asked them to meet Jesus, they had thought he was making fun. They had heard of the great new prophet. They knew how the people were flocking to him. "He will have no dealings with publicans," they had protested.

But Matthew had assured them that Jesus wanted to see them. And so they had come, half suspicious, half grateful.

As Jesus talked with them, he seemed to think of them as he would think of any other guests at any other table. Their suspicions died. They listened as he spoke. They responded to his friendliness, his goodness. They remembered the times they had cheated. They felt ashamed. "Can a tax collector be an honest man?" they asked themselves, surprised that they wanted to be honest.

Peter and Andrew and James and John felt uncomfortable. They did not know how to talk to the tax collectors. They were wondering what their friends would say if they should see them in such company. At last, the dinner was over. The disciples left as soon as they could get away. Outside the gate they breathed more easily.

But not for long. They saw men gathered there, some of whom they recognized. Isaac, the merchant, was there, and with him were other Pharisees.

Isaac bustled up. "Why is it that you eat with publicans and sinners?" he demanded. "I thought the Teacher might be a prophet sent by God. I was ready to hear him. But no prophet of God would eat with sinners."

The disciples said not a word. There was nothing they could say. In a moment Jesus came out. The light of the torch Matthew's servant held at the gate shone on the unfriendly faces turned towards him. He knew the men were despising those with whom he had eaten. He knew they were thinking how righteous they were to keep themselves away from sinful men who did not keep the Law. He answered their thoughts directly.

"You who are whole do not need a doctor," he said. "But those who are sick do need a doctor." And he walked away from them.

The disciples were disturbed by all that had happened during the evening. They were worried because Jesus had again made the Pharisees angry. As they walked home through the dark streets, Peter protested. "Teacher, is it wise to displease the leaders among our people?"

"Say on, Peter. What is in your mind?"

"We have made them angry at several places. We gathered grain and ate it on the Sabbath." He hesitated a moment, then went on. "You have healed the sick on the Sabbath. The Pharisees say we are setting aside our sacred Law, and teaching men to do so."

"But are we, Peter? Have we done evil on the Sabbath, or only good? Have we broken God's Law for the Sabbath?"

"No, Teacher, not God's Law. But the scribes have explained that obeying God's Law means observing all the rules they make for us."

"Just so, Peter. We shall keep God's Laws, and teach men so. We are not bound by the rules the scribes have added."

James was thinking about the scene at Matthew's gate. "We have offended them, too, by eating with publicans, Teacher."

Jesus turned sharply. "Yes, and in such manner we shall offend them often, James. They care more for keeping their customs than for helping men. But God cares more for men, all men." He was silent for a moment, then added more gently, "Do not let the Pharisees confuse you. Seek only what God would have you do."

CHAPTER XI

From Far Away

WHEN the news was spread about that Jesus had returned to Capernaum, the people again crowded before Peter's door. They had heard about the trip through Galilee. They remembered what they themselves had heard and seen in the synagogue at Capernaum. And so, in spite of being offended by the report that Jesus had eaten with publicans, the people came to him. More and more came, until the crowd was so packed in the courtyard and about the doorway that the people trod upon one another's feet.

As Jesus was teaching, he heard a noise above him. It seemed to be coming from the roof. He glanced up. The tiles of the flat roof over the house were being taken out. An opening appeared. And through the opening, a pallet, with ropes on the four corners, was being carefully lowered. A sick man lay on the pallet.

As the crowd stood staring at the strange sight, Peter hurried to Jesus. "It was the only way his friends could get the man through the crowd to you," he explained. "They asked if they could take him up the outside stairway and let him down through the roof."

Jesus looked into the eager faces in the opening above him.

"What good friends the man has!" he said to the people. "Their love and faith will help him."

The pallet now lay in front of Jesus. His eyes met those of the sick man. And the eyes told Jesus what the doctors had not been able to find out. They told him that the man's sickness was caused by his sins. They told him, too, that the man was sorry for his sins. And so Jesus said, "Your sins are forgiven. God loves you. There is no reason why you should be sick any longer."

The sick man gazed into the face of Jesus. He believed him! He believed that his sins were forgiven. Jesus spoke again. "Stand up now. You will be well."

And the man stood before the people, shouting joyously, "Thanks be to God! Thanks be to God!"

People crowded to hear Jesus the next day and the next. Each day there were more people than there had been the day before. The disciples grew tired, but Jesus seemed always ready to meet those who came. There was no longer room in Peter's street. The people gathered now in the meadow outside the town or by the seashore.

Late one afternoon a great crowd came to Jesus at the seashore, thronging about him. Suddenly he felt the water of the Sea of Galilee lapping over his sandals. He smiled toward Peter. "Can you get the boat, Peter? I am about to be pressed into the sea."

When Peter and Andrew brought the boat, Jesus stepped in, and the fishermen rowed out a little way. The people laughed as they saw what had happened. They became quiet again as Jesus taught them from the boat.

Peter and Andrew were keeping the boat steady with practiced hands, scarcely noticing what they did, for they, too, were listening.

Suddenly a man called out from the shore, "Teacher,

what must a man do to be ready for the Kingdom of God?"

Jesus recognized the man as a young lawyer, well known in the city for his love of arguing. He understood that the man did not ask the question because he was interested in the Kingdom of God, but merely because he wanted to debate with a teacher. But seeing the crowd about him, Jesus knew that even the man's dishonest question gave him an opportunity to teach the people. So he responded, "What are you taught? What does the Law say?"

The lawyer replied, "Why, the Law says, 'You shall love the Lord your God with all your heart and all your strength and all your mind; and your neighbor as yourself.'"

"You have answered your question. Do this, and you shall be ready for the Kingdom of God."

Now, the lawyer knew that the people had been displeased because Jesus had eaten in the home of Matthew, the publican. And so he thought he would embarrass Jesus by forcing him to say what he thought the Law meant by 'neighbor,' who was included.

"But, Teacher, who is my neighbor?" he asked.

Jesus thought for a minute. Then he said, "I will tell you a story." The people liked to hear Jesus tell stories. They listened eagerly as he began to speak, standing in the boat against the deep blue of the sea.

"A man was going from Jerusalem to Jericho and he fell among thieves. They beat him and took all his possessions, and stripped off his clothes. Leaving him half dead, they ran away.

"Now by chance a priest from the Temple came along the road. He saw the injured man, lying unconscious on the road. But he did not want to bother with a wounded man. So he crossed over on the other side and hurried past.

"A little while later a Levite came by, fresh from singing in the Temple service. He saw the man, lying in need. But

he was afraid the robbers might yet be about. So he crossed to the other side and went past as rapidly as he could.

"Then a merchant came by, a man of Samaria. He saw the man, wounded and bleeding. And though he was a Samaritan and the injured man was a Jew, he had pity on him. He dismounted from his steed, took oil and bandages from his bags, and bound up the man's wounds. Then he lifted him onto his steed and took him to the nearest inn, where he spent the night waiting on him.

"The next morning, when he had to leave, the Samaritan took out his purse and gave the innkeeper money to care for the man until he was well. 'Do whatever is needed,' he said. 'If this is not enough money, when I come by this way on my next journey, I will repay you.'"

As Jesus finished the story, the people were still, thinking. They watched the lawyer when Jesus asked, "Which of the three men was neighbor to the man who fell among thieves?"

The lawyer was in a hard position. But he knew that he dared not refuse to answer the question while all the people were waiting. He said rather surlily, "Why, he who took pity on him."

"Yes, you have answered rightly. And if you would fulfill the great commandment and love your neighbor, you will do as the Samaritan did: show mercy to anyone who is in need."

The people did not like the Samaritans, but they had liked the Samaritan merchant in the story. They were pleased with the answer Jesus had given the lawyer.

As they left the sea, flaming now in the red and gold of sunset, and started toward their homes, many believed that what Jesus taught was true, and they decided to become his followers.

It was late before Jesus and the disciples reached Peter's house. The disciples were tired and hungry. All day they had been so busy that they had scarcely had time to eat.

After the evening meal, Jesus talked with them about needing more helpers. "You have accepted Matthew as one of you now," he began.

Peter broke in. "Yes, and a good worker he is, too, Teacher."

Jesus smiled. "I am glad, Peter. But even with Matthew's help you are too busy. I shall choose some others soon to help us."

When he had said good night, Jesus walked away from the house toward the hills. He wanted to be alone with God. As he thought of many of the men who had become his followers, he asked God to help him choose some of them to go with him as his helpers. All the night he spent praying.

Early the next morning he came again upon the road leading to Capernaum, rested and ready to choose his helpers. He was thinking of them, planning the special work each one might be asked to do. His thoughts were interrupted when he saw a man walking toward him, leaning heavily on a staff. "How tired he seems," Jesus thought. "He must have come a long way. From a distant place." The man drew nearer. As the two came face to face, the man dropped his staff and stared at Jesus. "It is you! My playmate in Nazareth!"

"Simon! All Nazareth mourned you as dead!"

"I was as dead for all these years."

"Yet you are alive! And here in Galilee!" Jesus gazed at his friend, marveling that he had escaped the massacre at Sepphoris. But his quick eyes saw that Simon was almost fainting from weariness.

"Come, Simon, let us rest under the tree yonder." With his arm around the exhausted traveler, Jesus led him to a tree by the roadside, and spreading his cloak as a pallet, urged Simon to rest. He brought water from the wayside stream, and some figs which had fallen from the tree, and waited while Simon rested and refreshed himself.

"Now, tell me all about it."

Simon the Zealot leaned back against the trunk of the tree, closing his eyes for a moment. He shuddered as if remembering the horror through which he had lived.

"I escaped from Sepphoris," he began. "Even now I dare not tell you how. I could trust no man. A price was on my head. I lived like a wild beast. Finally I made my way into Phoenicia, and there I have been ever since. Now I have come back to Galilee, hoping the Romans think that I am dead."

"Probably they do, Simon. They are proud of their power and would like to think none can escape it. But you have escaped it."

Simon nodded, then winced with pain. Jesus stood up in quick concern. "Your feet are bleeding."

He brought fresh water from the stream and bathed the bruised feet. Then for a while they talked of Nazareth. But Simon was troubled, and soon he was speaking again of the country.

"I heard many rumors as I traveled, but I dared talk with no man. Tell me. How is it with our country?"

Jesus answered directly. "The Romans are still here, Simon, and they rule sternly."

"Is Herod Antipas, the puppet king, still holding onto his part of his father's kingdom?"

Jesus nodded. "He rules in Galilee, and continues to build cities and palaces."

"With the tax money our poor people have to pay," Simon responded bitterly. "And in Judaea? Is it true that a new governor has been sent from Rome by Caesar?"

"It is true, Simon. A Roman governor is still over Jerusalem. Pontius Pilate is his name."

"The rumors tell of a hard and cruel man and one who has no respect for our religion."

The two friends fell into silence, each thinking his own thoughts about the country he loved so much. Then Simon spoke. "You were right, Jesus. You were right about the Zealots. A few poorly armed men against the mighty legions of Rome! We said you were a dreamer, but you knew more than we did about the cost of battles." His voice came haltingly now. "You always thought there was a better way to save Israel than the way of the sword. Have you found that better way?"

"I know now, Simon. Men will be saved and they will save Israel when they repent of their sins and become good men, loving God and loving their neighbors. When they are ready for the Kingdom of God."

Simon shook his head. "I do not understand you." He looked searchingly at his friend. "Tell me, is it true? What I have heard of you as I came through the country?" He hesitated. "That you are a prophet?"

Jesus' eyes were steady and kind as he met the questioning gaze. "Come into the city with me, Simon. You may decide for yourself."

He helped Simon to his feet, gave him his staff, and they walked toward the city, Jesus slowing his pace to that of his tired companion.

CHAPTER XII

The Meadow and the Sea

WHEN Jesus and Simon reached Capernaum, Jesus told the disciples all about his boyhood friend. Simon was made welcome and invited to rest at Peter's house until he regained his strength.

As Simon listened to the others talk, he marveled at what he heard of the work Jesus was doing among the people.

A few days later, feeling rested, Simon went with the disciples to a meadow outside the city where those who had become Jesus' followers were gathered. Jesus went up onto a little hill, and the people came around him, and he spoke to them.

"Blessed are you bceause you want to be ready for the Kingdom of God," he said. "You have set your hearts on God's way, the way of love and right dealings with others. You are grieved because there is wickedness and cruelty in the world, but your mourning will be comforted. Blessed are you because you have trusted God and have not followed the way of the sword. Blessed are you because you have sought to be ready for God's Reign by living peaceably with other men, by forgiving those who are unkind to you, by doing good to others."

He went on to tell them what they were to do. "There are those who say that I have set aside the Law. Do not think I have set aside the Law of God. No, I have come to tell you what God's Law requires of you. It is more than following the letter of what is laid down, as the Pharisees do. You must be more righteous than they are."

His followers spoke among themselves. "How can this be?" they asked. "The Pharisees observe every law."

Jesus answered their question. "The Law says that you are not to kill. But I tell you that God requires of you not even to be angry with others or to speak evil of them.

"The Law says that if a man injures you, you may do to him just what he has done to you, an eye for an eye, a tooth for a tooth. But I tell you that God requires you not to take any revenge at all. Instead, do good to him who has harmed you. Let this be your rule, to treat everyone you meet just as you would like to be treated by others.

"The Law says that you are to love your neighbor. But I tell you that God requires that you love also your enemies, and pray for those who mistreat you.

"And do not judge others. Let God be the judge. Think, rather, of your own faults and how to overcome them. Neither do good works to make a parade of your virtue before men. If you give a gift to someone in need, do not blow a trumpet to tell the world you have done a good deed! Instead, give your gift secretly. And when you pray, do not stand in the market place and call attention to your piety, but go to a place apart and God will hear your prayer."

When Jesus stopped speaking, a man in the gathering said to a friend, "How different his words are from those of the scribes!"

"Yes," the friend agreed, "the words he speaks sound as if they come from God rather than from man."

But Jesus was asking them all to listen again. While they stood quietly in the field, he called from among them twelve men. When they had come to him, he asked them to go with him as he traveled through the country and be his helpers. There were the five who had already been with him: the brothers, Peter and Andrew, and James and John, the sons of Zebedee, and Matthew, the publican. Now he asked Simon the Zealot to go with him, and six others: Philip and Bartholomew, Thomas, James the son of Alphaeus, Thaddaeus, and Judas Iscariot.

The people who had become followers of Jesus knew most of these men. And they said to one another that they were glad Jesus had more good helpers.

That evening the twelve disciples came to Jesus at Peter's house and they talked together. None of those chosen was an important man, but each of them could help and they all wanted to go with Jesus. Some of them had special gifts or skills. Peter seemed the natural leader, the one who could speak better than the others. Matthew knew how to keep records. Philip could choose provisions and supplies, and Judas was a good treasurer. So these men each took his own special work.

Jesus knew that these helpers themselves needed to be taught. Even though the crowds seemed always to be about them, he often took the twelve to a quiet place where he could answer their questions and talk with them about the Kingdom of God.

There were some women, too, who wanted to be helpers. There was Susanna, a widow of Capernaum, whose child Jesus had made well; and Joanna, whose husband worked in Herod's palace; and Salome, the mother of James and John; and Mary Magdalene, whom Jesus had saved from a miserable and sinful life. These and some other women asked to help. They could not go into the villages with Jesus and teach as the disciples did, but they could prepare food for their journeys and mend their garments, and help take care of the many sick persons who came to them.

Thus with his special helpers Jesus was able to reach more people. He and his disciples became known throughout all the country as a band which went about doing good.

After a time Jesus felt that the disciples were ready to go into the villages without him. So there came a day when he sent them out, two by two, to different villages, while he stayed in Capernaum.

Some days later, as Jesus was waiting for the disciples to return, he was talking with the women helpers. Suddenly he was interrupted by a man running toward him. He recognized the man as one of the disciples of John the Baptizer.

"What is it?" he asked as the man threw himself, exhausted, on the ground.

"John the Baptizer—"

Jesus waited.

"John the Baptizer is dead."

"Dead? Did Herod Antipas—?"

The man nodded, unable longer to control his weeping. "Herod had him beheaded."

The women heard the news in horror. Jesus put his hand gently on the shoulder of John's disciple. "I know how you grieve for John. He was a great man, a true prophet of God."

When the messenger had recovered, he spoke anxiously. "Teacher, we fear for you also." The women clung together, trembling, as he went on. "Rumors have come from Herod's court. He has heard of the crowds who are listening to you. It has come to us that he has sent spies to watch you."

As Jesus stood silent, Mary Magdalene moved away from the other women and ventured to address the messenger.

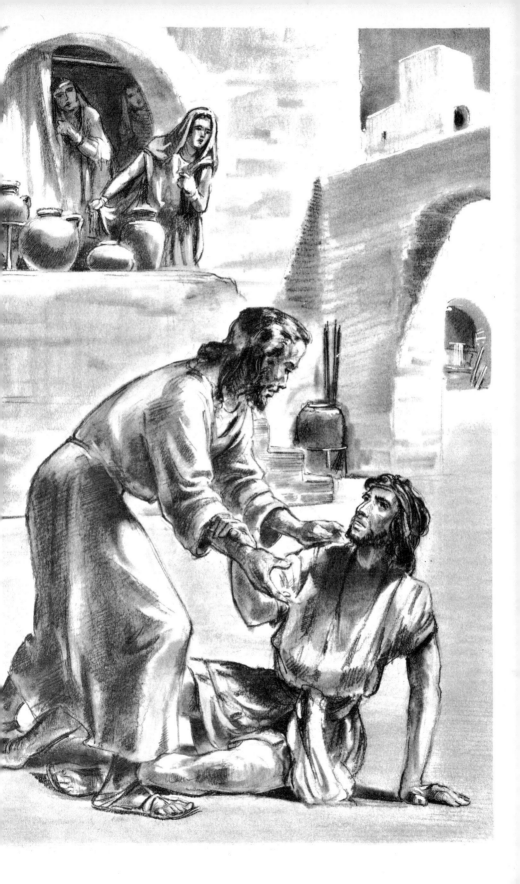

"But, sir, why should Herod seek to harm the Teacher? What has he done amiss?"

"Herod fears the Teacher, woman. He fears him because the people follow him. He fears him lest the people should seek to make him their king, in Herod's place."

"King in Herod's place?" Mary Magdalene repeated. "Why—"

John's disciple was listening to her no longer but was urging Jesus to flee from Galilee. The women talked nervously among themselves. "Could it be?" Susanna wondered aloud. "Could it be that the people would seek to make Jesus king?"

Joanna spoke in a frightened voice. "It is true that he has spoken of the Kingdom of God, but he has said nothing of Herod's throne."

Salome was thinking of her two sons, who were disciples. "Israel is looking for a leader to deliver her from the Romans. If Jesus should become king—"

Mary Magdalene turned her eyes away from the women toward Jesus. And she knew that Herod was wrong. Jesus was not thinking of setting up a kingdom in the place of Herod's. "No," she began. Then she remembered that the messenger had said Jesus was in danger. He must get away! As she was wondering what she could do, she saw Peter and Andrew hurrying down the street, returning from the village where they had been preaching.

"Teacher, the people heard us gladly," Peter began eagerly. He saw the disciple of John the Baptizer, and paused questioningly. But Andrew, who had known John and loved him, ran toward the man. "Tell me, what has happened to John?"

The two men were deeply shocked when they heard that John the Baptizer had been killed. But John's disciple was urging them to think now of Jesus.

"He also is in danger," the man told them.

As Peter and Andrew tried to plan what they should do, Jesus continued to stand silently, thinking and praying.

Soon others of the disciples returned. When they were all about him, Jesus spoke to Peter. "Get the boat, Peter. Let us go over to the other side of the Sea of Galilee. All of you are tired. Come away and rest awhile."

Andrew went with Peter to make the boat ready. The others followed to the shore, where the women handed Philip some food they had prepared and then left them to go back to the city.

In the meantime, the people of Capernaum heard that the disciples had returned from their journeys and that they had been well-received in the villages of Galilee.

"Soon the whole country will be following Jesus," the people said enthusiastically. "Just see how crowds are coming to Capernaum from all parts of Israel. From Judaea and from beyond Jordan, and even from the countries round about Israel. There was never a prophet like Jesus!"

Someone reported that Jesus and the disciples were going toward the sea, and people turned in that direction.

When the boat was ready, Jesus and the twelve disciples climbed on board, the fishermen set the sails, and when the people reached the shore, the boat was far out on the water.

The day was clear and the sea was calm. It was peaceful on the water. Jesus closed his eyes and went to sleep. But the disciples' thoughts were disturbed. John the Baptizer had been killed. Simon especially seemed sure that Herod and the Roman officers were now watching Jesus.

"John's disciple is right," he said. "Herod is fearful and jealous. He thinks Jesus may take his throne. And the Roman officers do not like to see the people crowding around any teacher. They fear he may stir up a rebellion."

"Well, perhaps Jesus will," Judas said boldly.

"But the Teacher does not talk about rebellion, Judas," Peter responded as he gave the ropes a tug. "He tells us to love men; he does not tell us to fight them. Not even the Romans. Don't you remember, James, that he even carried a Roman soldier's pack once, to save a boy who was about to refuse the order?"

"Yes, I remember. But I have never understood why he did it."

"Nor have I," John agreed. "Surely he must plan some way to save Israel from the Romans."

"He plans to save Israel, John, but not by fighting Romans. Of that I am sure," Simon answered earnestly.

There was little wind, and the boat was moving slowly northward across a corner of the sea, toward a secluded place in the hills which the fishermen knew. When they reached the shore, and had beached the boat, Peter stood uncertainly, wondering if they should awaken Jesus. But Jesus spoke to them. "How quiet the fields and the hills are! It is good to be away from the city for a while."

As they left the boat and started toward their retreat, Peter pointed toward the south, calling out sharply, "Look!"

The disciples saw people coming around the shore of the sea. Crowds of them were coming, the reds and blues and yellows of their cloaks brightened by the afternoon sun.

Simon spoke quickly. "Do not stop, Teacher. Go ahead to the retreat. We will follow after we send the people away."

"Yes, Teacher," Peter urged. "Go ahead and wait for us. Such crowds are dangerous, when Herod's spies may be watching every move."

But Jesus was looking at the people. They were nearer now. He saw that some of them were bringing sick persons to him. Others were hurrying anxiously, as if they needed him. He could not leave them.

Soon the people were all about him, and he welcomed them. The disciples followed him, but there was uneasiness in their faces as their eyes scanned the crowd.

"Do you suppose we can recognize Herod's spies if they are here?" Peter asked Simon.

"Whether we recognize them or not, I am sure they are here. They will need only the smallest excuse to arrest the Teacher."

He stopped abruptly. "And there," he said in a tense whisper, nodding toward a man Peter did not know, "there is more than a slight excuse. That man is a leader among the Zealots." His eyes darted here and there. "And there are other Zealots with him, several of them." His voice dropped even lower. "It looks as if they have decided that Jesus is the one they have been seeking as leader—as king. They may act now."

"What!" Peter looked as if he could scarcely believe that Simon was serious. "Do you mean they may call upon the people here to make Jesus king? In Herod's place? Or even in Caesar's place?"

But Simon was serious. "Yes. And such a move is just what the spies are looking for."

Jesus was in the midst of the crowd, speaking to those who sought him, comforting those who were sorrowful, ministering to the sick ones, feeding the hungry, while the disciples helped as they were needed. But Simon and Peter stood apart, watching closely. They saw the Zealots gathering one little group, and then another, speaking to them excitedly. The people were responding with enthusiasm. Yes, the Zealots were stirring up the people to make Jesus king! Peter, too, was sure of it now.

He was terrified. "We must get him away. Quickly." He started impulsively toward Jesus. But Simon held him back.

"The people around Jesus all know you too well, Peter. Stay

here and watch. Let me go. Maybe they will not notice me."

Attracting as little attention to himself as possible, Simon came near enough to touch Jesus on the shoulder. He spoke softly and cautiously. "Those who would stir the people to revolt are here. They will seek to make you king."

Jesus' eyes, which had been on those who needed him, now flashed alertly over the crowd. He saw what was about to happen. It must not happen. Leaving the disciples with the people, he moved quickly toward the woods. As Jesus passed out of sight, Simon found that his knees were trembling.

The Zealots knew that the people were ready now, ready to call upon Jesus to be their king. They ran a little way up the hill, then turned toward the people with shouts of acclaim on their lips. But where was Jesus? He had been standing just there. Now he had disappeared. Though they sought him in the crowd, they could not find him.

Soon the people realized that Jesus had gone away. They grew restless. "Perhaps we were wrong to try to make Jesus our king now," they said to one another. "Perhaps he knows best." Uneasiness began to take the place of enthusiasm. "Perhaps Roman spies are here," they whispered among themselves. The crowd broke up, and soon the people were returning to their homes.

When the Zealots knew that Jesus had slipped away, they were baffled and angry.

"Why does he hide himself?" one of them asked. "The people are ready to follow him."

"Yes; with his power to draw the people and our secret swords, we could have started a movement to free Israel. Now. This very day."

"He says he is a true son of Israel. Why will he not let us make him our national leader?"

"Maybe he thinks the time has not yet come, that we should

wait longer. Wait! How long we have waited!" They shook their heads as they started back to the city.

In the quiet place apart, Jesus thought over what had happened. It was clear that those who heard him were not understanding what he was saying to them about God's way to save them. How easily the Zealots had stirred the people to think of him as a national leader, come to deliver them by the sword. The sword of Israel against the sword of Rome! How foolish it was!

Even the disciples seemed not yet to understand. Jesus was sure he needed more time to teach them, away from the crowds. Perhaps it would be better to take the twelve out of Galilee for a while so he could have more time alone with them.

When the disciples came to him, he did not talk with them about the Zealots. He said only that they would go back to Capernaum.

CHAPTER XIII

A Foreign Land

Early next morning Peter was awakened by a hammering on the door.

"What is it?" he called.

"News from Jerusalem," came the answer. "Terrible news. Hurry."

It was indeed terrible news that Peter was told. Some men of Galilee had gone to Jerusalem to offer sacrifices in the Temple. It had been reported to Pilate, the Roman governor, that these men had come to the capital city to start a revolution, and he had ordered soldiers to capture them. The soldiers pursued the men to the inner court of the Temple itself. Angered that pagan soldiers had entered the sacred Temple, the Galileans had tried to force them out. And the soldiers had fallen upon them with the sword and had slain them all. Slain them inside the Temple.

Peter sent for the other disciples and told them the news. Their thoughts flew to Jesus. They all knew, now, that he was in grave danger. Herod Antipas, the puppet king of the Romans, had put John the Baptizer to death; Pilate, the Roman governor, had slaughtered the Galileans. It was clear beyond any doubt that the Romans were sternly determined to kill anyone who seemed to them likely to gather a following among the people.

During the day the disciples made among themselves many plans to protect the Teacher, but when they came to tell the plans to Jesus, they hesitated. He knew as they did that he was in danger; he would decide what to do. They could only wait anxiously.

When he called them together in the evening, they felt sure that he had made a new plan. "Let us leave Galilee for a while and go to Phoenicia," he said.

"Phoenicia!" James exclaimed. "Why, Teacher, that is a land of the heathen."

"Perhaps the heathen land will listen, James."

Simon was thinking of Herod and his threat to Jesus. "In Phoenicia we will be outside Herod's realm," he whispered to Peter. "This is a good plan." And he began talking about the journey.

"We will need some money. Judas, you have the moneybag. Do you have enough?"

Judas questioned Philip, who had charge of the provisions. "What will we need to buy?"

"The women will provide us with bread and dried fish for the journey, as they have done before. We can find fruit along the way. We shall need to buy but little."

Judas shook his head. "You are forgetting, Philip. We are going to Phoenicia. There will be no fruit to be picked up from the ground as there is in Galilee. And there will be few friendly householders to offer us shelter. I think we should not venture so far without more money."

"Do not be troubled about the money, Judas," Jesus said. "We shall need but little." He smiled as he added, "The Pharisees chide us for being common men. Let us show them that common men are sturdy."

And so Jesus and the band of twelve made their plans and started on their way. As they walked along, they had often to step off the busy road to let a caravan pass. While they waited, resting in the shade of the cedars, Jesus would teach them, seeking to help them understand the Kingdom of God.

When they came into Phoenicia, they found that some travelers into Galilee had brought back word of the new prophet. Thus there were many who were eager to hear the words of Jesus and to bring their sick to him. So Jesus spent some weeks in the foreign land, ministering to those who needed him, and teaching the disciples.

He had been thinking and praying about his country all the time he had been in Phoenicia. Now he was ready to go back. He knew he might be arrested. Instead of becoming afraid and cautious, he had decided to speak more boldly. So Jesus and the disciples turned again toward Galilee.

As they drew near to Capernaum, the people came out to meet them, crowding about them in glad welcome. A man ran up and said, "Teacher, I will follow you anywhere."

His excited face told Jesus that the man was thinking only of following a popular preacher and wonder-worker. So he said seriously, "The foxes have holes and the birds have nests, but I have no home."

The people standing near heard what Jesus said. Of course, they had known that he had no home, that he was staying with Peter when he was in Capernaum, and that when he traveled about the country, he sometimes was invited to spend the night with his followers, and sometimes slept out in the fields. But as they had heard him, they had come to think that he was more than a prophet; that the time would come when he would have not only a home but a palace. Now, as he spoke, they felt puzzled. Could he mean that he always would be poor? That he was not to be a leader with palaces

and soldiers and power? That they had been mistaken about him?

At that moment a man in the crowd called out, "Teacher, tell my brother to divide his property with me. He has received more than his share from our father's estate."

Jesus answered directly. "Who has made me a judge over your property? Beware of covetousness! Take heed that you think not too much of the things you possess, for a man's life does not depend upon riches. Think rather of the Kingdom of God and how you may get ready for it."

A man in the crowd scowled as he spoke to his neighbor. "Now why didn't the Teacher do as the man asked him? There is nothing wrong about wanting to get what is one's own." But Jesus was speaking again, and the neighbor turned to listen.

"Any man who would prepare for the coming of God's Reign will have to think first of what God would have him do. Not first of what is good for his business, nor what will make the largest profit, nor even what is best for his own family. He will have to think first, always, of what is God's way for him."

The people were listening, but they were wondering. They had often been told that God rewarded good men by making their fields yield good crops and their business prosper. Many of them thought that riches were a sign of God's favor, and meant that men were happy. Did Jesus think this was not true? As if he had heard their question, Jesus answered.

"No, it is not riches that make a man happy. So do not store up goods and money for yourselves on earth. Do you not remember how the moths destroy your fine raiment? And how rust ruins your vessels? And how money in your house tempts thieves to break in and steal?"

His eyes fell upon the poorly clad people on the edge of

the crowd. They were not thinking of storing up possessions; they were wondering how they were to get bread for their children day by day. Jesus spoke to them.

"God knows you need food and clothing for your children. Try not to worry about these things. God wants you to have what you need." His hands swept out toward the meadow. "Think of the flowers blooming here all about us." Plucking a brilliant red blossom he held it before them. There was a lilt of gentle laughter in his voice as he asked, "Could even the greatest king in all the world have a robe dyed to match this color? No. Not even Solomon in all his glory was arrayed like one of these blossoms."

He spoke tenderly now. "If God so clothes the flowers of the field, will he not much more care for you? Think first of getting ready for God's Kingdom of love and righteousness, and the things you will need will be yours."

Jesus turned again toward the scribes and Pharisees. "God wants men to have what they need," he repeated. "But do not burden yourselves with possessions. They will only make you anxious. Rather cause men to love you by doing good to those who need your help. Be kind to little children; forgive those who wrong you; help your neighbor when he is in trouble or has too much work to do. This is God's way for men. And those who walk in it will be happy."

The scribes and Pharisees listened scornfully. "This man teaches foolishness," Isaac, the merchant, said to a friend beside him in the crowd. "It is well enough to care for those in need and to help one's neighbor. There are laws which tell how it should be done. But the laws do not forbid men to store up possessions for themselves."

"No. Nor do they say that a man must always be forgiving," the friend added.

Isaac was frowning. "More than that, the Law says it is a

man's duty to keep himself from touching all uncleanness. Yet this man would set aside our sacred customs with his zeal for the sick and the hungry and the poor, who are often unclean. Bah! He is no prophet. He is a dangerous man, stirring up the people to think they are so important in the eyes of God."

One of the leading citizens of Israel, whose name was Nicodemus, had listened to Jesus for many days. Now as he heard the Pharisees talking, he protested.

"No mere trouble-maker could do the good deeds Jesus has done among the people." Then he faced them squarely. "And a man seeking his own advantage would try to win your approval, the approval of men of influence, not spend his time with the poor and the outcasts."

His fellow Pharisees turned upon him. "Would you, too, follow the fellow?" Nicodemus was silent.

Jesus saw the scribes and Pharisees talking together. Now he spoke directly to them. "Woe unto you, blind guides of the people! You are careful to observe all the religious customs. You set aside a tenth part of your harvest as a gift to God. But justice and love and mercy to the children of God do not concern you. It is to these matters that you should give your attention, along with making your tithes.

"Woe unto you, pompous men! You love the front seats in the synagogue and you love to be greeted respectfully by the people who pass you in the market place. You make a parade of your fasts and your prayers to be seen by men. But you are not humble before God.

"Woe unto you, hypocrites! For you speak proudly of your observance of the Law, of keeping yourself untouched by uncleanness, of following the ceremony in washing your hands and your vessels. But inwardly you are full of secret sins and impurity."

He stopped a moment. The crowd was listening almost

breathlessly. How did the Teacher dare to speak so to the Pharisees? They were the most important men in the city!

Moving a few steps nearer to his hearers, Jesus continued more sternly. "You even set aside the Law of God for your own law. God's Law says that you shall honor your father and mother and care for them. But there is one among you who says, 'This money I would use to care for my old parents, but I have promised it to God, and so I may not use it as I choose.' By your hypocrisy you let your parents be in want and set aside God's Law."

The people gasped. They knew, indeed, that a prominent Pharisee had let his parents be in want, just as Jesus had said. But that anyone should dare call it out in public!

"I tell you," Jesus went on, "unless you repent and mend your ways, you will be judged by God as surely as any publican or common man whom you despise. God does not look upon the outward manners of a man, but upon his heart."

The people had so often been rebuked by the scribes and Pharisees for not observing all the laws and the ceremonies. Now, they were not a little pleased that these leaders were being so plainly taken to task.

But the scribes and the Pharisees were enraged. Isaac, the merchant, spoke for them all. "The man must be silenced. He must be put out of the synagogues. Now."

"Upon what charge will you have him silenced?" Nicodemus asked. "That he dared to say God would punish our secret sins?"

"If you wish to follow this fellow, Nicodemus, that is your affair. But leave us to deal with him," Isaac retorted.

"Come. Let us not be hasty in the matter," Nicodemus went on in a more friendly manner. "The man spoke disrespectfully of us, yes. But is there not, perchance, some truth in his words?"

"I say let us act without delay. The man is dangerous." Isaac stopped a moment as if he was making up his mind. When he spoke again it was in a positive voice. "Let us go to the Sadducees."

"Go to the Sadducees? Come now, Isaac," his friend said to him, "we Pharisees need not humble ourselves before those haughty men who work with the Romans. Surely this Jesus has sent you out of your mind."

"I tell you again, the man is dangerous. He will turn the people against us, their true leaders. They will forsake our sacred traditions. You saw how they hung on his words. To make common cause with the Sadducees is better than to let the man go freely about speaking such false doctrines."

The Pharisees moved away from the crowd, talking among themselves, as Jesus continued teaching the people. After a while he saw them returning.

"Teacher," one of them called out, "if we would hear you further, we must know whether you are sent by God. Therefore, show us some sign of God's favor. Show us some miracles that we may know God is with you."

Jesus saw the trickery in their faces and knew they had been planning to try to turn the people against him. He answered promptly. "The Kingdom of God is not to come with signs and wonders, but with righteousness and love and mercy. Listen to my words and repent and do good, even as the people of Nineveh listened to the words of the prophet Jonah and repented. Thus will you know that God sent me."

Strangely enough, the people seemed not to turn from Jesus because he did no wonders at the command of the Pharisees. And when the Pharisees saw their plan had failed, they went away to seek other means of silencing Jesus.

The disciples were worried. Why had Jesus spoken so harshly to the men who were leaders in Capernaum? They knew that many of these men, prominent in the councils and in the synagogues, were pompous men, proud of their knowledge of the Law and of their piety. And some of them were hard in their business dealings. But they were men of power and influence, and most of them were considered upright men and deeply religious. Was it wise for Jesus to turn them against him?

Peter decided to try again to persuade the Teacher to speak more gently so that these men would continue to listen. He turned with the words on his lips.

But Jesus was speaking again. The people were eager to hear him continue to criticize the important men. Instead, he was speaking now to them.

"All of you who follow me and prepare for God's Reign may have to suffer, even as I shall have to suffer. When you set your hearts on God's way, many will turn against you, because God's way is not the way of men. They will call you 'foolish ones.' They may even put you out of the synagogues as heretics and persecute you."

His hearers whispered among themselves. "Why, Jesus speaks as if there are those who would oppose the Reign of God."

"Have not all men been waiting these weary years for the time when God would save us from our oppressors?"

"Why should any man be made to suffer or be put out of the synagogues for preparing for the Reign of God? What could he mean?"

Jesus continued. "God's Reign will not be a kingdom as this world knows kingdoms. It will not give honor to riches and power and mighty swords. It will be a kingdom of good men who love God and live together as God wants men to live."

Seeing that the people were bewildered, yet trying to understand, Jesus went on. He drew pictures for them in words.

"I will tell you what the coming of the Kingdom of God will be like. It will be like the gathering of all the people before a king. And the king will separate the righteous from the unrighteous. And he will say to the righteous, 'Come, enter the Realm of God. For I was hungry and you fed me, I was thirsty and you gave me drink, I was a stranger and you took me in, I was cold and you clothed me, I was sick and you took care of me, I was thrown into prison and you feared not to visit me.'

"Then shall the righteous say to the king, 'Why, when did we see you hungry and fed you? Or thirsty and gave you to drink? When did we see you a stranger and took you in, or cold and clothed you? When did we see you sick or in prison and ministered to you?'

"And the king will say to the righteous, 'I tell you that whenever you showed mercy and kindness to one of these brothers of mine, even the least among you, you did it to me.'

"But to the unrighteous ones the king will say, 'Begone from me. You have no place in my Kingdom. For when I was hungry and cold and sick and lonely and in prison you did not care for me.'

"And the unrighteous will say to the king, 'But when did we see you hungry or cold or sick or lonely or in prison and did not look after you?'

"And the king will say to the unrighteous, 'I tell you that when you refused to help one of my brothers in his need, even the least of them, you refused to help me.' "

As Jesus stopped speaking, the crowd stood for a moment wondering. Was this really what the Kingdom of God was to be?

The Zealots who had been listening to Jesus now moved away. "Does he think feeding the hungry and taking care of the sick are more important than freeing our nation from Rome?" they asked one another angrily.

Many of the people who were not Zealots but only patriotic men of Israel were disappointed that Jesus taught so little about making Israel a great nation, and so much about doing good to others.

"Who can spend so much time thinking of the needs of other people?" they asked one another. "Who can turn away from good profits in his business to ask if someone is hungry? Or sick? Or lonely? Jesus is a good man, but he is a dreamer. What he asks men to do is not practical." And many who had been following him went away and did not come back again.

There were others in the crowd who knew that Jesus had himself done what he was telling men to do. He had helped their sick, he had fed their hungry ones, he had been a friend to the lonely, the outcasts, the discouraged ones. Now as he told them the Kingdom of God would be a kingdom of the kind, the merciful, the righteous, they understood something of what he meant. They, too, had thought God would send a leader to free them from Rome. But they knew little about all that. Here among them was one who cared about them as he told them God cared about them. They would not leave him.

But the scribes and Pharisees were more opposed to him than ever before. Not only did they think that what Jesus taught was wrong, but now he had dared denounce them before the people. When they had tried to discredit him, he had instead discredited them. They were angry. When Isaac pressed his plan, no one longer opposed him. They would go to the leaders in Jerusalem. They would go to the Sanhedrin itself. Jesus must be silenced.

CHAPTER XIV

Toward the Mountains

Troubled as they were by what had been happening, the disciples wondered how they could persuade Jesus to avoid stirring up the enmity of important men.

"He is in danger from the Roman authorities," Peter said. "He will need all the support he can muster among our own people."

Simon nodded vigorously. "You are right, Peter. He is in danger."

"You can see that the crowds are smaller." James spoke in a worried voice. "I have noticed that many people who had been coming to him have stayed away for the last few days."

Judas held up the moneybags. "These are lighter, too. Fewer men seem to want to help us travel about the country these last few weeks."

"I will speak to him this very night," Peter promised himself and the others. "But now, we must go to help him. Though the crowd is smaller than it was, there are yet many people there in the field with him."

A short time after Jesus began talking to the people, the disciple heard some confusion. They saw some mothers with little children trying to make their way through the crowd.

"Now, why are those women bringing children here?" James asked impatiently. "We have enough troubles without children to interrupt Jesus."

"So many people have gone away angry, we must not let these children disturb those who are left," John added.

"Well, then, why don't you tell the mothers to take the children back home?" Peter demanded, his temper short with worry. "Here, I will go myself and send them away."

He strode toward the women and the children, stern-faced and annoyed.

"Wait, you women, take the children home. They are interrupting. Can't you see the Teacher is busy?"

"But," one of the women began timidly, "we wanted the children to see him! We thought, perhaps, he might—"

Peter did not let her finish. "Well, there are too many people here. He has important work to do. He cannot be disturbed by children."

Jesus noticed what was happening. He stopped talking and made his way through the crowd. The children saw him coming toward them and stood still, shrinking against their mothers. They had been frightened by Peter's rough words. Even the mothers looked frightened.

Jesus smiled at them all. "Come," he said, taking one of the older children by the hand. "Let us get away from the crowd." He nodded toward an oleander tree full of flowers. "We will go over there in the shade." Peter stalked along behind, disapproving.

When they had reached the pleasant shade, Jesus sat down on a big rock. He reached out his arms and all the children ran toward him. They knew he wanted them! And while the people waited, Jesus and the children talked together.

After a while Jesus turned to Peter. "Never send the children away when they come to see me. I want them always to

be welcomed. They belong to the Kingdom of God." Peter was angry and hurt and ashamed all at the same time. He stood for a few minutes watching Jesus with the children. Then he started back to the other disciples.

The crowd was growing weary. The sun was hot. The people were puzzled by much that Jesus had been saying. So they began to drift away toward their homes.

When only a few stragglers were left, the disciples found a shady spot and sat down on the ground to wait for Jesus. They were feeling discouraged. As Peter joined them, James spoke the question that was in all their minds. "Why does he offend the Pharisees, who might contribute much to his cause, and spend time with children?"

Peter threw himself down on the ground. "I wish I knew why. Yet," he hesitated, "yet, he seemed happy with the children. You should have seen his face."

"But if he is to be the leader of Israel, he must win some important men to be his followers," Judas insisted. "Some men who have influence in the councils of the land, in the Sanhedrin at Jerusalem."

"I wonder why he doesn't see that," John said angrily. "I wonder—" He stopped as Peter gave a sharp exclamation and pointed.

"There! The man coming toward us. Now, if only he could be won as a follower of Jesus."

The others sat up quickly. The man coming toward them was one of the younger leaders in the councils. Rich and handsome, he was also a Pharisee who was highly regarded by all the people as a man of honor and goodness.

Jesus was telling the mothers and children good-by. Peter looked anxiously toward him, then made a move as if he would try to persuade the Teacher to speak gently to this young man.

But Jesus was striding toward them now, looking as if he had put aside his cares for a moment, and had been enjoying the company of those he loved. He seemed rested, his eyes were smiling. Peter stood still.

The young man, seeing Jesus leave the children, began walking toward him. And so Jesus and the rich and influential young leader met face to face. They stood so for a long moment.

Jesus felt drawn to this Pharisee as to a friend whom he could love. The smile with which he had left the children did not fade from his face. He greeted the young man warmly and the greeting was returned. But the visitor seemed to know just what he wanted to ask and he put the question at once.

"Good Teacher, you talk of the Kingdom of God as a kingdom of love and righteousness. Tell me what I must do to be ready to enter the Kingdom of God."

Jesus remembered the young lawyer who had asked a similar question for the sake of an argument. How different the question seemed as this man asked it!

"You know the commandments. They tell you the righteous way God wants men to live."

"Yes, all the commandments I know. And I have kept them since I was a boy," the young man replied. But his face and his voice showed that he knew he had somehow missed finding joy and happiness.

Jesus saw the rich clothing the man wore, the rings on his fingers, the gold chain about his neck, the jeweled girdle. He knew that to the young man possessions were very important. Too important.

"It is your possessions that are in your way."

The young man showed his surprise. "Why are possessions a hindrance, Teacher?"

"Because you think of them too much," Jesus told him.

"You worry too much about your possessions. You wonder if they are safe. You plan how you can protect them, how you can add to them. They are keeping you from thinking of God's way for men, of understanding other men and knowing how to help them."

Jesus knew better than the disciples did that this was a man who could be a real helper. He wanted the young man to come with them, to be one of them. Yet he must make clear to him what was necessary.

"You are righteous in your dealings, but those who would get ready for the Kingdom of God must love God and their fellowmen more than they love their possessions."

As Jesus looked into the face before him, his eyes were kind and full of understanding. "This is not easy when one has great possessions. So, sell your possessions and give the money to those who need it." There was warm friendliness in his voice as he added, "And when you are free of your possessions, come with me—come, and win men to the Kingdom of God."

Jesus heard the angry mutterings of the disciples. But he was thinking only of the young man. He so wanted him to come!

The young man was drawn to Jesus as he had never been drawn to any one. What Jesus had said about the Kingdom of God had made him feel that life could be better, happier, than he had ever known it to be. He hated the cruelty, the greediness, the oppression he saw about him. He wanted to be a good man himself and to live among good men. He longed to go with Jesus, to help men as he had seen Jesus help men, to see joy come into their faces in the place of sorrow and fear.

But even as he longed to be with Jesus and help men, the thought of leaving his possessions filled his mind. How could he give them up? The beautiful things in his home which he cherished? The soft raiment that touched his skin? The comforts his money bought for him? The servants to wait upon him? No, he could not give them up. He could not!

Gazing at Jesus sorrowfully, he shook his head. A moment later, he walked away.

Jesus stood watching the young man until he passed out of sight. "How hard it is for one who loves possessions to enter the Kingdom of God!" he said.

Behind him the mutterings of the disciples came more clearly.

"The young man could have kept his money, and brought it to us," Judas complained to Philip. "With more money in the moneybags we could do more good." He shook his head. "Though I have been with Jesus for many months, I do not understand him. He turns away those who might help his cause and make our lot easier. It seems as if he does not want to become a great leader of Israel."

James whispered to Peter. "Why don't you tell him now? That he must not turn away the men who have influence?"

Peter took up the words of Jesus. "But why should it be so hard, Teacher, for a man with great possessions to prepare for the Kingdom of God? Such a man can persuade other men to follow him. He can do many good works."

"Yes, he can, Peter. But the love of his possessions so often becomes more important to him than the love of God," Jesus answered. "His possessions fill his thoughts, and in caring for them he forgets to care for people who need him."

He saw they did not understand, though they were trying. "Come, you are weary. Let us go to our rest."

Long after the others were asleep, Jesus was praying. He knew the disciples were confused and unhappy because men were turning away. Perhaps they, too, would like to go away. He must find a way to be alone with the disciples for a while. So the next morning he proposed again that they seek a place where they could be alone.

Once more they entered the boat. This time they sailed to the northern end of the Sea of Galilee, toward the high mountains. The day was calm, and Jesus talked with his disciples as they crossed the blue waters. They left the boat on the northern shore and walked along the path which followed the Jordan River through rough country thickly overgrown with trees and bushes and cut with deep ravines.

It was a lonely way. They met no travelers, and the disciples listened as Jesus taught them.

Toward sunset Jesus walked ahead, thinking of what he wanted to do before they returned. Judas spoke to Peter. "You said little last night about not offending the Pharisees," he reminded him. "Isn't this a good time to speak plainly?"

Peter seemed uncertain, not positive as he had been the night before. "Yes, I suppose it is. But I wonder—all that he has said—" As Peter hesitated, Jesus stepped back toward the disciples. He asked a direct question.

"What are men saying about me? Who do they think that I am?"

The question startled them, and for a moment no one spoke.

Judas looked at Peter as if asking why he did not say what he had agreed to say. James seemed to be expecting Peter to speak out, too. As he remained silent, James spoke almost angrily. "Well, Teacher, the Pharisees say you are not a good Israelite. That you do not keep the Law. I have heard that they are trying to have you put out of the synagogues."

"Probably they will succeed, James," Jesus replied. "But what do other men say?"

Andrew remembered what one of the disciples of John the Baptizer had told him. "Why, some men say that you are

John the Baptizer, risen from the dead. I have heard that Herod himself thinks so."

Jesus waited.

"I have heard men say that you are the prophet Elijah come back to earth, because you are not afraid to tell important men that they have sinned," Simon told him.

"And I have heard it said you are the prophet Jeremiah," John remembered.

"Oh, they say all manner of things, Teacher," Matthew added. "Most of them seem to think you are one of the old prophets come to us again."

Jesus let his eyes rest for a moment on the snow-covered peak of Mount Hermon ahead of them. When he spoke again to the disciples his voice was very quiet, but his face showed them how important their reply would be.

"But what do you think of me? Who do you say I am?"

While the others had been talking, Peter had stood looking at Jesus almost as if he were seeing him for the first time. The words of rebuke which he had been about to speak seemed frozen inside his throat. Now as the others were silent, wondering what to say, Peter spoke without any doubt. "You are the Christ, the one sent by God."

Jesus' face seemed to reflect the sun on Mt. Hermon, so radiant did it become. "Blessed are you, Peter, because you do not doubt me. Though many men have turned against me, yet you believe in me. God himself has shown you the truth."

The other disciples knew, too. Whatever men might say, whatever they themselves might wish Jesus would do or would not do, they knew that he was not like other men. They knew that Jesus was sent by God.

They walked on toward the mountains.

Judas seemed full of excitement. "This may be the turning

point," he said to James. "Jesus may now declare himself our leader against Rome."

"Perhaps he will declare himself our leader, Judas. But I think he will not be like warrior leaders."

The others were quiet, each one thinking his own thoughts about Jesus.

As the sun went down behind the mountains, the ravine grew dark and chill. When they came to a small inn, the travelers asked for shelter for the night. Weary from the long walk, the disciples soon fell asleep.

Jesus was thinking of what Peter had said. He knew the disciples did not yet understand what God wanted him to show to men. But they believed he was sent by God. That made all the difference!

Because they believed in him, he could tell them about the time of testing that was before them. For Jesus knew now that he would have to stand against the leaders of his own country. They were not willing to accept God's way to save Israel.

The Pharisees were angry, and he had lost the support of almost all of them. But he knew, too, that God's way must be made known among men. No matter who opposed him, men of Israel or men of Rome, he would speak for God.

He decided that now he must go toward Jerusalem, the city of King David of old. The city where the powerful Sadducees lived, where the Sanhedrin met, where the Roman soldiers were gathered in the great fortress of Antonia, where the thousands of pilgrims came from many lands to worship in the Temple. There in Jerusalem he would call all the people—the rich and the poor, the men of the city and the men of the provinces, the men of high position, and the lowly ones—he would call them all to prepare for the Reign of God.

He would help the disciples to be ready for the dangers

that lay ahead. He would leave the results in the hands of God. Having made his plan, he fell asleep.

The next morning, as Jesus and the disciples were ready to start back to Galilee, he began to speak of his plan. "Let us go into Judaea, toward Jerusalem."

Simon gave a start. He knew better than the others how dangerous it would be for Jesus in Jerusalem. "Is it wise to go to Jerusalem?"

Jesus did not answer him. He was thinking of what he should say to the disciples. "Let us go to Jerusalem," he said again. "There I shall suffer many things. I shall be accused by the Pharisees and by the Sadducees. I may be delivered to the Romans." He stopped. Yet it must be faced. He must face it. The disciples must face it. "I may be put to death."

"No!" Peter sprang up. "No, Teacher, do not speak so! You are sent by God. Men can not harm you."

"You do not see as God sees, Peter, but as a man sees. Do not try to hinder me. You have said I am sent by God. And so I am. I must do the work God has sent me to do, in Galilee and in Judaea and in Jerusalem."

CHAPTER XV

On the Road to the Great City

THOUGH the disciples were afraid for him, they knew they dared not oppose Jesus further. And so as soon as they had returned to Capernaum, they set about making the necessary preparations for the journey to Jerusalem.

"By which road shall we go?" Philip asked. "The road beyond Jordan or the road through Samaria?"

James spoke up quickly. "Samaria is a land of outcasts. Let us go over Jordan."

"If we go through Samaria we will not be likely to find any followers who will provide food and shelter," Judas reminded them. "Food and shelter require money, and the moneybags are not heavy."

"But through Samaria is the better route, Judas," Thomas said.

"Yes," John agreed. "But how Samaritans hate Jews!"

"And how Jews despise Samaritans!" Matthew countered briskly.

Jesus had said nothing while the disciples were talking about the route. Now they turned to him. "What do you say, Teacher?" Philip asked. "Which route shall we take? Through Samaria or beyond Jordan?"

"Let us go through Samaria, Philip. It will be better so." He smiled. "You are a good provision man. You will find food and shelter for us, I am sure."

"I will do the best I can, Teacher. But since the crowds going to Jerusalem for the feast days will be so large, Judas and I will go ahead a day's journey, and make arrangements for you and the others."

In spite of their concern for Jesus' safety, the disciples began to feel excited at the thought of going toward the capital city. When the morning came for them to start, they put aside their fears and worries. Jesus must be mistaken. Surely God would not let any harm come to his chosen prophet. Thus they took the road toward Jerusalem.

When evening came they found themselves near a village, and as soon as they entered its streets, a man came to them to say that Jesus was to be entertained at his house overnight, and the disciples in the houses of some neighbors. "Philip and Judas came yesterday, and found many homes eager to receive you, Teacher," he told them. So Jesus and the disciples ate the evening meal and spent a restful night among friendly people in the Galilean village.

During the next day they crossed over into Samaria. The people here were not friendly, for the Samaritans had nothing to do with the Jews. They turned the other way when they passed the pilgrims going to Jerusalem. It was growing late in the evening when the disciples saw a village ahead of them. "It must be here that Philip and Judas have made arrangements for the night," James said.

"I hope so," John answered. "But I see no messenger looking for us."

They walked on for a few minutes. "It is strange that no one comes to meet us." There was a note of uneasiness in James' voice. 'We have come a long way today. It is time for food and rest." He peered anxiously down the twilight road. Then he called back in relief, "Here come Philip and Judas. They must have found a place for us."

But as the two messengers came nearer, James saw that something was wrong. He and John ran forward. "What is it? Aren't we to stay here?"

Philip's face was dark with anger. "No!" he shouted. "The people here will not let us stay. They turned us away from every house."

John spoke in rebuke to Judas. "But they would have let us stay at the inn for money. Why didn't you offer them money? It is late, and the Teacher should have rest."

"I did offer them money," Judas retorted. "They even refused money."

"The Samaritans seem to hate us most when we are on our way to Jerusalem for the feast days," Philip muttered, as if to explain his failure.

James was furious. "So they refused us shelter! We came as friends. Yet they even refused our money for the food we need." He turned to Jesus. "Teacher, call down lightning upon this village! Let it be burned up!"

Jesus looked at his disciples, so angry and full of thoughts of revenge. "Would burning the village provide us with food and shelter, James? Or cause the Samaritans to be friendly?" He shook his head. "No. That is not the way." He knew the disciples were tired and hungry, and that Philip felt unhappy because he had failed to find a place for them. He spoke now confidently. "Let us go on to the next village. It is not very far. I am sure they will receive us." He took the lead and walked with so light a step that the disciples were ashamed to say more about being tired. They followed him to the next village and there they found the food and shelter they needed.

Early the next morning they were again on their way. Out of Samaria, now, they entered Judaea and found friendly followers to greet them as they journeyed. In the afternoon they came into the prosperous city of Jericho, with its gardens of flowers and orchards of fruit trees and groves of spicy balsam. A large crowd gathered about them, the people eager to see and hear the new prophet whose fame had reached them.

Near the edge of the crowd a small man was standing on tiptoe, straining this way and that. Though his clothes showed that he was a man of wealth and position, the people near him all tried to keep from touching him. His neighbors despised him. He was Zacchaeus, a publican, head tax collector for the Romans in all that district.

Zacchaeus seemed not to notice that the people were trying to avoid him. He had heard about Jesus from some fellow taxgatherers in Capernaum who had been invited to Matthew's party. When he had learned that Jesus was in Jericho, he had left his office and hurried into the street. But because he was so short, he could not see over the crowds. Jesus was moving on now, the throng following, moving in the direction of Zacchaeus' own house.

Quickly the publican ran ahead of the procession and climbed into the branches of a large sycamore tree. He was gazing down intently when Jesus turned his head and looked straight into Zacchaeus' eyes. The attention of the crowd was attracted. They began to laugh at the tax collector peering out among the leaves of the tree.

"What sent you into the tree to see the Teacher, Zacchaeus?" someone called out.

"Why, with all the fine food your Roman friends supply you, one would think you would be a big, strong man. Yet, behold, you are so small of stature that you have to climb a

sycamore tree to be as tall as other men," another jeered.

But Zacchaeus was paying no heed to the crowd. His eyes were fixed on the face of Jesus. What he saw there made him sure the other tax collectors had told him the truth. Jesus did not scorn them as other men did. While the thought was passing through Zacchaeus' mind, Jesus spoke to him.

"Come down, Zacchaeus, and make ready to have company. For I would like to stay at your house tonight."

As they heard the words of Jesus, the people drew back. Their friendly manner changed. They began to complain to the disciples.

"I was going to invite the Teacher to my home," Jacob, a prosperous Pharisee, said to Peter. "I should think that a prophet would know Zacchaeus' reputation. The people of Jericho all know it."

"Why, he pays bribes to the Romans!" another man called.

"And cheats his own people!" someone else shouted.

Peter shook his head wearily. How he wished Jesus would ask his advice about such matters! He spoke to Jacob. "I am sorry about not going to your house, but the Teacher does not turn away from the tax collectors. He feels that he should try to help all men to repent and mend their ways."

The Pharisee walked away angrily. Most of the crowd followed him, leaving only a small group watching as Jesus and the disciples went toward Zacchaeus, who welcomed them gladly to his home.

Jesus saw how the people hated Zacchaeus, but as they walked through the beautiful gardens to the house, he did not reproach the publican for dealing unfairly. Zacchaeus himself was remembering all the people he had cheated. As long as the people had scorned him and hated him, it had not seemed to matter whether he was honest or dishonest. He had collected more than the tax which was fixed by law, and had kept the money to make his house more beautiful, his gardens more spacious, his moneybags heavier. Now it was different. Jesus had not scorned him, but had been friendly. Jesus had not expected him to cheat, but had expected him to be honest.

"Teacher," he began hesitatingly. Then he rushed on. "Teacher, I am sorry I have taken more than the fair tax." Being sorry was not enough. He must make amends.

"I will find those from whom I have taken more than the fair amount of tax and I will pay back all I have taken unfairly." He paused. "I will pay back more than I have taken. I will pay back—" Zacchaeus hesitated a moment. "I will pay back four times as much as I took!"

Now he could face the Teacher. Now he was an honest man once more. He had promised to make amends.

Jesus gave him a friendly smile. "Yes, Zacchaeus?" There was a question in his voice, as if the Teacher was expecting something more. His eyes swept the beautiful gardens, the magnificent house. They came again to Zacchaeus' face. "Yes, Zacchaeus?"

Zacchaeus understood. It was not enough to give back what he had taken unfairly. Not even if he gave back more than he had taken. He must give something that was his own. He must not only be honest; he must be generous. He felt light-hearted, almost gay, for the first time in years. He was going to give away, instead of take away! He laughed out loud. Then he spoke seriously.

"Yes, Teacher, I will do more than give back what I have taken. I will give half of all I have to help those who are in need."

The people standing just outside the garden heard what Zacchaeus was saying. "Can this be Zacchaeus, the publican, speaking?" they asked one another. "Will he give back what he has taken? Will a tax collector give away his money?"

They listened as Jesus spoke. "You have repented and have made amends, Zacchaeus. You love God and love your neighbors. You are ready for God's Kingdom of righteousness." The Teacher and the publican, followed by the disciples, passed into the house, leaving the crowd staring.

The next morning, trusting Zacchaeus to carry out his new plans, Jesus and the disciples went on their way toward Jerusalem. As they left Jericho, they came into almost desert country. In the hills above the road, they saw some shepherds watering their sheep at a well, and wondered how they found pasture for their flocks in such barren land.

It was very hot. There were no trees along the way to give them shelter from the sun. Crowds of pilgrims going up to Jerusalem thronged the hot, dusty road.

When Jesus and the disciples stopped to eat the noonday lunch which Zacchaeus had prepared for them, the only shade they could find was a sort of cave in the rocks. Pilgrims gathered around, asking Jesus questions.

In the crowd were some Pharisees who had been in Jericho and had been offended because Jesus had gone to the home of Zacchaeus. They seemed annoyed now as they saw the people listening to him eagerly, even in the burning heat. They complained to one another, and Jesus overheard them. How could he help them and the people gathered around him to understand that God cared for all men, the publicans as well as the Pharisees? He remembered the shepherds they had seen in the hills. All the people would understand about a shepherd's care for his sheep. So he spoke to them.

"What man among you, having a hundred sheep, and having lost one, does not leave the ninety and nine, and go after the one which is lost until he finds it? And when he has found it, does he not lay it gently on his shoulders and

144

take it home? And when he is home again, does he not call his neighbors to come in and rejoice with him because he has found his sheep that was lost?"

The people knew that Jesus had described just what happened. How often they had seen shepherds come in, worn out, their clothes torn by thorns, their hands cut by brambles, but their faces glad because, safe in their arms, was a sheep or a lamb which had been lost.

Jesus turned directly toward the Pharisees who were complaining about his being friends with Zacchaeus. "I tell you that even so there is joy in the heart of God over one man who has done wrong and who repents and seeks to mend his ways."

He spoke now to all the people. "Each of you is precious to God. He seeks you all, as a shepherd seeks his sheep, to bring you into his Kingdom."

"Can it be that the righteous God forgives sinners, Teacher?" someone called out to him.

And Jesus told another story.

"There was once a man who had two sons. The younger son said to his father, 'Father, give me now what will come to me as my share of your property. I would like to go to another place to live.' And so his father gave him his share of the family money. And the young man went into a far country. There he fell into the company of spendthrifts, and he squandered all his money in foolish and sinful living. Then there came hard times in that country. The man became poor. He was hungry. He went to another man's farm and asked to take care of the swine so that he might eat, even the refuse which was fed the swine.

"One day the young man came to himself. He said, 'I will go back to my father. I will tell my father that I have sinned against him and that I am not worthy to be called his son.

I will ask my father to let me be only a servant in his house.'

"And so the young man started home to his father. When he was yet a long way off, the father saw him, and ran to meet him. The son said, 'Father, I have sinned against you. I am no longer worthy to be called your son. Let me be a servant in your house.'

"But the father called to his servants to make ready a feast of welcome. 'We will rejoice, because this my son, whom I had thought dead, is alive and home again.'"

Jesus finished the story and the people felt comforted. "Since God loves us and forgives us, surely we can trust him," they said to one another.

"We need not worry so much about the Romans or about ourselves. If we try to be good and to do good, God will help us and take care of us."

As they continued along their way, the people were talking about Jesus and praising him.

"He has done many works of mercy among the sick in my city," a merchant of Capernaum told those near him.

"He speaks plainly and tells stories so that the people can understand him," a man from beyond Jordan said.

"He tells men to repent," a Judaean shepherd remembered. Then he added, wonderingly, "You heard him say God loves us as a shepherd loves his sheep, and will forgive us as a father forgives his son."

A carpenter nodded. "And he says it does not matter if one is poor and unimportant among men. Every man is important before God."

"He tells us we should not worry about how we are to get on. If we do what God wants us to do, God will take care of us," a farmer said.

A Galilean camel driver had listened to all that was being reported. "Yes, but does he say how we will be delivered from our conquerors? Does he say when the Messiah will come to save us from the Romans?"

"Jesus says all that is in God's hands. Our part is to do good and trust God," an old man answered confidently.

The camel driver spoke again, this time hesitantly, as if almost afraid to say what was in his thoughts. "Do you suppose—could he, himself, be the promised leader, the Messiah sent by God to save us?"

Many of the people, remembering all they had heard about Jesus, began excitedly to wonder if this prophet in their midst was indeed the leader who would deliver them.

The disciples heard what the people were saying. They pushed away the memory of what Jesus had told them about his suffering and death. They would not think of the warning he had given them, again and again, that he was not to be a leader to rule over men. Or even of what they themselves knew of the danger he faced in going to the capital city. They were swept along with the growing enthusiasm of the crowd. Jesus was going to Jerusalem, the city of King David! Would he set up his kingdom there, as God's chosen one?

Only Simon tried to calm them. He knew too well what this excitement might mean. He knew too well how closely the Roman soldiers would be watching the crowds gathering for the feast days in Jerusalem. But when he tried to remind the other disciples of what Jesus had said, when he tried to persuade them to calm the people, they brushed him aside impatiently.

"The people have accepted him," James insisted.

Judas spoke more boldly. "He may declare himself king, in Jerusalem."

"Judas!" Simon rebuked him sharply. "To speak such words endangers the Teacher. The very rocks along the roadside may have ears."

John seemed more interested in the enthusiasm of the crowd. "Don't you see? The people are ready to follow him. Now. Today."

"Let them alone," Peter demanded. "Let them do the Teacher all honor. If he enters Jerusalem surrounded by followers, the rulers will know that he has the support of the people."

"But a leader with a large crowd of enthusiastic followers —don't you understand, Peter?" Simon protested. "Not even after what happened when the Zealots tried to declare him king? Demonstrations are what the Romans are watching for. They will say he is enlisting followers for a revolt."

But Peter and the others would not heed his warning, and Simon followed the crowd with fear in his heart.

As they journeyed, they came to the Mount of Olives. There were trees growing here, and the people began gathering branches along the way. They would need them in the ceremonies of the festival days. Now as they approached the city, they began to sing the songs of their faith. Singing and waving their branches, the pilgrims rounded the Mount of Olives, and there the Holy City stood before them. The city where King David had established his kingdom. The city where the great Temple shone in the sun.

Here in their midst was the strange new prophet. Surely he was sent by God! Suddenly there seemed to sweep through the crowd an upsurge of zeal for their God. He was the God of their fathers. The God of Abraham, the God of David. He was a God of love and righteousness and power. And they were his people. Jesus was right, God would save them. This prophet spoke to them in the name of God! He was sent by God!

The crowd was pressing around Jesus now. He knew these people were ready to accept him. He would enter

Jerusalem amid joyous followers. And all those who opposed him would hear of it. Soon would come the final conflict.

James came forward leading a donkey. "A friend sent his donkey. We told him you needed it."

As Jesus mounted the donkey, the people began waving their branches and singing:

"Hosanna!
Blessed is he who comes in the name of the Lord!
Blessed be the Reign of God to come!
Hosanna! Hosanna!"

And so Jesus came again to Jerusalem.

CHAPTER XVI

The Temple Court

O<small>N THE DAY</small> Jesus was entering Jerusalem, a group of the leading men of Israel, including Caiaphas, the high priest, had gathered in an inner room of the Temple and were disputing among themselves about him. Isaac, the merchant of Capernaum, had carried out his purpose. He had brought his questions about Jesus and his teachings to the chief men of the country.

Nicodemus spoke in defense of Jesus. "I have heard him often as he taught the people. I have seen his deeds of mercy among the sick. He speaks as a prophet, and I am persuaded that he is a prophet."

"But I understand that he is a man of the common people, untaught in the schools, unlearned in the Law," a Pharisee from Jerusalem objected.

Isaac spoke up. "That is true. He is an unlearned man who dares dispute with the scribes. I myself have heard him hold them up to ridicule before the people in Capernaum."

"Was it ridicule, Isaac?" Nicodemus asked. "As I heard it, he called certain men of standing hypocrites because they put the observance of forms and ceremonies before justice and mercy to others."

"Whatever he said in Capernaum," the Pharisee from Jerusalem insisted, "he is making the people discontented with their leaders. We hear reports from all over the country that he has criticized the scribes and Pharisees for demanding strict observance of the Law." The speaker seemed deeply disturbed. "Why, men must observe the Law. Israel must hold fast to the customs that keep her people separate from others. Else our nation is lost, and become as the heathen nations round about us."

"You are right," Isaac agreed. "And on many occasions Jesus has even broken the Sabbath, and led other men to do so."

"What has he done on the Sabbath that has not been done to help men, Isaac?" Nicodemus spoke earnestly. "One day I heard him call upon the scribes and Pharisees to answer plainly the question, 'Is it right to do good on the Sabbath?' And none of them dared to tell him it was wrong." He turned to the others. "No, my friends, Jesus does not break the law of the Sabbath. He shows men how to use the Sabbath for helping men."

"Fie! How can you speak so, Nicodemus?" Isaac demanded. "And what do you say of his eating with publicans? He even has a publican in his band of disciples: Matthew, the tax collector of Capernaum."

Jacob, a Pharisee from Jericho, had later news of associations with publicans. "Just a few days ago he passed through Jericho. And he spent the night in the house of Zacchaeus, the notorious publican. I myself saw him go there. Yet I told one of his disciples that I was ready to invite the Teacher to my own home."

"I grant he associates with publicans," Nicodemus admitted. "He says they need him. And he does seem to make them over into decent men. Tell me, Jacob, is it true what I have heard about how Zacchaeus has changed his ways?"

Isaac interrupted. "That is beside the point," he blustered. "The man Jesus is dangerous. Dangerous to our sacred institutions. Dangerous to our leaders, who have spent all their lives studying the Law that they may please God by keeping it, and teach men so."

Caiaphas, the high priest, had been sitting aloof and silent. He and the other Sadducees thought the dispute among the Pharisees about a wandering prophet from Galilee was rather foolish. These aristocratic men of Israel, favored by the Romans, and leaders of the Sanhedrin, the governing body of the city, had listened with little concern. But though the Pharisees disapproved of the manner in which the Sadducees worked with the Romans, they recognized them as important men in the Sanhedrin, and they knew they had to have the support of the Sadducees whenever any matter came before that body.

Isaac saw that Caiaphas had not been interested. He must say something which would stir the high priest. So now he added, "Yes, Jesus is dangerous to Israel herself!"

"Dangerous to Israel, Isaac? How so?"

"Why, he disturbs the people," Isaac answered carefully. He wanted to say just enough to win the support of the Sadducees in silencing Jesus. "He teaches false doctrines. Yet the crowds follow him and hang on his words."

Now Caiaphas' question came quickly. "Does he create disturbances?"

Isaac saw the direction the high priest's thoughts were taking. The Romans granted the Sanhedrin a large amount of authority in local affairs, and in return, they expected that order would be kept. The Sadducees were alert to any threat of a disturbance, because it was a threat to their own position and power. A disturber of the peace must be arrested, and at once. Isaac, the Pharisee, was not ready to go so far. He became cautious.

"I would not say he caused disturbances. But he leads the people astray. He leads them to expect that God will save them, even if they do not observe all the laws. He leads the common people to feel that they are too important in the eyes of God."

Caiaphas' brief interest seemed to be slipping again into boredom. "Surely the scribes, whose business it is to teach the Law, do not need to be abashed by this fellow. Surely they can hold their own before the people."

"But he has bewitched the people. He has a manner of speaking to which they give heed."

"Well, what would you do about him?" the high priest asked impatiently.

Isaac spoke positively now. "He must be silenced! He must be put out of the synagogues. Those who follow him must be put out of the synagogues and made as strangers in Israel. The people must know that he is a false prophet, to be scorned, not trusted."

"Then see you to it. I have important matters demanding my attention. I must leave you," and the high priest turned toward the door.

At that moment the sound of singing in the street came into the room. Caiaphas stood still.

"What is that?"

A young man ran to the window. "Some pilgrims are waving palm branches and singing," he reported.

"Why are they behaving in so unusual a manner as they come to the Temple?"

But the reporter now spoke in a tone of excitement. "There he is! It is Jesus on the donkey in the midst of the crowd."

The men hurried to the window. They saw the crowd, the waving branches, and Jesus in the midst. They heard the joyous singing. They sensed the enthusiasm.

"You see what I mean," Isaac remarked. "The people are bewitched by him."

The high priest was frowning. "Such demonstrations are not approved. I will report this disturbance to the Roman officer lest it may become a riot."

"Wait!" Isaac did not want the Roman officer called in. "After all, it is a religious demonstration," he said slyly. "The Romans have granted the high priest authority to deal with religious matters."

Caiaphas was annoyed. Clearly he was caught between two difficulties. If he took charge of the situation, he might offend the Romans. If he failed to take charge, he would seem to yield his own authority.

"I will speak to the fellow," he announced and strode out, his robes fluttering behind him. He summoned a messenger whom he sent to bring Jesus to his house.

But when Caiaphas stepped out of the Temple court, he found the city full of excitement. "Who is this?" people were asking as they hurried toward the procession.

"Why, he is Jesus, a mighty prophet," someone answered.

"Where is he from?"

"From Nazareth in Galilee. And he speaks in the name of God and does wonderful works of mercy."

"A prophet? From Nazareth? How can that be?"

Pondering what would be the wisest course for him to follow, Caiaphas stood watching the people. They seemed enthusiastic, yes. But some were questioning, too. And none seemed in the temper for a riot. Perhaps it would be wiser to wait. If he silenced the man now, it would certainly cause trouble with the people. And he did not want trouble with the people on the eve of the festival. It might become serious.

While Caiaphas was watching, undecided, Jesus slid off the donkey easily, and walked toward the Temple. The high priest could see his face now. No, it was not the face of a fanatic. It was calm and gentle. "There seems to be no danger from the man," he reasoned. Nevertheless he hurried back to the Temple court and took a position where he could see but not be seen.

He saw Jesus enter the outer court. Though the crowds followed closely behind him, most of the people seemed to be going about their own business. Here was a group from a distant country going to the money-changers to get their foreign money changed. Here was a group going to the dove merchants to buy birds for their sacrifices. Here was a man buying a lamb, and here was another talking with the cattle merchant about a burnt offering.

Caiaphas let his attention wander from the prophet of Nazareth. He was watching the merchants. They seemed to be doing a good business, an excellent business. The large crowd of pilgrims would mean a good profit. The high priest rubbed his hands in satisfaction. For the Temple priests owned the booths in the Temple court which the money-changers were using, and rented them for a high fee. Caiaphas had a large interest in the dovecotes where the doves were bred for the sacrifices, and in the cattle farms where the sheep and cattle were made ready for the burnt offerings. Yes, he would make an excellent profit from this festival season.

He seemed not to be disturbed by the din in the outer court—the merchants shouting their wares, the clanging of the money as the coins were tested, the bellowing of the cattle. The noise, the dust, the confusion seemed to concern him not at all. Near by, he heard an argument between a money-changer and an angry pilgrim from a far-distant land.

"You would cheat me, you merchant of Satan," the pilgrim shouted. "I will die of hunger before I return to my home. You would take all I have. All I have."

The money-changer laughed slyly. "But what will it profit you to spend your money for the journey to Jerusalem if you do not pay the Temple tax? And you know full well your tax will not be accepted by the priest unless it is made in the proper coinage."

Caiaphas hugged himself. Yes, it was a profitable business!

At that moment he heard a voice. Above the din and confusion of the Temple court, above the bellowing of the cattle and the clang of the coins and the hawking of the merchants, above all the noise he heard the ringing words. "It is written, my house shall be called a house of prayer, but you have made it a den of robbers!"

There was a sudden hush. The hawkers were silenced. The money-changers held onto the coins poised for testing. Even the cattle seemed quiet. And out of the quiet came the sound of tables being overturned, of coins falling this way and that. Then there was a rushing of great bodies, and the cattle, loosed from their stalls, ran into the streets. Above the heads of the people, doves, freed from their cages, were flying about.

The people stood dumfounded. They saw Jesus standing in the midst of the money-changers and the merchants, denouncing them, overturning their tables, loosing their animals and doves. How did he dare? They knew the stalls were owned by the powerful Sadducees. How did Jesus dare to defy them?

Then they seemed to realize what he had done. He had rebuked these men for making profit out of the worship,

their own worship of their own God. For making them pay high rates of exchange for the money they offered to God. For using the very Temple of their God as a market place.

They crowded around Jesus in joyous enthusiasm, praising him and singing hosannas.

Jesus spoke again. "A house of prayer," he said quietly. "The Temple of God shall be a house of prayer."

The high priest was beside himself, as he hurried to the conference room.

CHAPTER XVII

The Conference Room

W<small>HEN</small> Caiaphas entered the room, his blazing eyes and crimson face told the others that something serious had taken place. They rose with one accord. "What is it? What has happened?"

Almost too angry to be understood, Caiaphas poured out the story of what he had seen in the outer court of the Temple. Jesus had dared to denounce what he, the high priest, and the chief men of the country had done. He had denounced them in the name of God. Before all the people. And the people had sung his praises for condemning the practices of their high priests.

Aghast, the others listened. Nicodemus thought exultantly, "The courage of the man! The glorious courage! To defy the Sadducees at the very center of their authority. And how they deserved this rebuke. The temple markets are a disgrace to Israel." Then he thought more soberly, "The Sadducees will never forgive him for this. Never."

Even the Pharisees unfriendly to Jesus were moved by his courage. Secretly they were not a little pleased that the haughty Sadducees had been publicly denounced. But they, too, knew that the matter of silencing Jesus now was out of their hands. When he interfered with the Temple profits, he stirred all the Sadducees from indifference to determined enmity. Nothing now could stop them. They would silence him, and promptly.

The high priest was so full of rage at what he had seen that he was in favor of calling the Temple guard to arrest Jesus at once. But though the situation was serious, some of the Sadducees counseled caution.

"Clearly, the man is not an ordinary wonder-worker," one of them said. "He speaks fearlessly, and there is authority in his voice and bearing."

Isaac spoke, not without a certain satisfaction. "The people seem to be supporting him in his charges against the money-changers and the Temple merchants."

Caiaphas' lips curled in scorn. "The people! Bah! Say, rather, the accursed rabble."

"Yet this rabble are sons of Abraham, come to the Temple to make their sacrifices to God," Nicodemus reminded him. "And upon their taxes and offerings the high priest and all his assistants depend for their—uh—very comfortable—living."

"To arrest him now, just after he has done a spectacular act which the people approve, might arouse them so that there would be a riot," cautioned another Sadducee. "A riot is a riot to the Romans, whether caused by a prophet stirring up the people or by the high priest arresting a prophet."

To this last argument Caiaphas gave heed, though unwillingly. The last thing he wanted was to cause a riot.

"Suppose," proposed Jacob, "instead of stirring up the people, we turn them against this Jesus. Suppose we trap him with questions which he cannot answer without betraying himself to be the ignorant man he is."

"Or else showing plainly that he is plotting a revolution," a Sadducee added.

Those scribes and Pharisees who had heard Jesus in other cities were secretly doubtful that he could be trapped as easily as these men thought. Nevertheless, they consented to the plan. And so the men set themselves to devise trick questions to ask Jesus before the crowd.

While the leaders were plotting thus against him, Jesus had quieted the people. He was walking back and forth between the great pillars, away from the confusion in the center of the Temple court. Here he was speaking of the Kingdom of God, and ministering to the sick who were brought to him. Many people asked him questions and he answered them, sometimes with a story, sometimes with a direct reply.

Now a man eased his way through the crowd until he stood near Jesus. He began in an oily voice, "Teacher, we know that you are sincere and that you teach the word of God fearlessly. You do not court human favor. Now, tell us, is it right to pay taxes to Caesar, the Roman emperor, or not?"

All the people listened intently. This was a question which had been burning in their minds for a long time. The tax was the sign of Roman power over them. It kept them poor. They hated it, and more than one riot had been caused because of refusal to pay it. Only the powerful influence of the Sadducees kept the people from fresh riots.

Seeing the trickery in the man's face, Jesus knew the question had been asked to embarrass him. If he answered, "Yes, pay the tax," the people would think that he had betrayed their hopes for freedom; that he, like the Sadducees, was a collaborator with the Romans. If he said, "No, do not pay it," the leaders could call the Roman authorities and have him arrested for telling the people to revolt. Yet he did not hesitate for an answer.

"Show me a coin used for paying the tax," he commanded.

The man held out a small silver coin. "Tell me," Jesus went on, leaving the coin in the man's hand, "whose likeness is on the coin? By whose authority was the money made?"

And the man answered, as he had to answer, "The emperor, Caesar's."

"Then give to Caesar what belongs to Caesar," Jesus said, but added solemnly, "and give to God what belongs to God."

The questioner did not know what more to say. He dared not ask the other questions the rulers had given him.

The people, seeing that the man had been silenced, were pleased, though they were not sure what Jesus meant. But the Zealots spoke angrily among themselves. "He should have answered 'No'," one of them said. "No man can be a good Israelite and pay taxes to Caesar."

The messenger returned to the conference room and reported what Jesus had answered. "The man speaks not as other men speak," he added.

The rulers denounced their messenger roundly for his failure. "See to it that you do not make us think that you, too, are one of his followers," they warned.

Then they made another plan to throw the followers of Jesus into confusion. He spoke much of forgiveness. "God forgives you whenever you repent," he had said over and over. But suppose one should be brought before him who had been caught in a serious sin for which the Law of Moses required a certain punishment? Would he teach men to break the Law and not punish the one who had sinned? Or would he deny his teaching of forgiveness?

Thus it came about that while Jesus was teaching, some men were seen pushing their way through the crowd, half dragging a woman after them. Because of the commotion they created, Jesus stopped speaking. Now the men were directly in front of him. The woman lay huddled on the

ground in shame and misery, not daring to raise her eyes.

"Teacher, this woman has been false and unfaithful to her husband. Now, the Law of Moses requires that such a one be stoned. What do you say?"

Jesus read in the faces of the men their meanness of spirit and their plan to use the woman to confuse him before the people. The woman raised her eyes for a moment, and he saw in them her suffering. He must save the woman and help the people to understand. He stooped over and began making marks as if he were writing on the ground. Everyone was still. The people wondered how he could answer.

Suddenly Jesus faced the men. "Let the one among you who has never sinned himself cast the first stone," he commanded, his clear, strong voice carrying to the very last person in the crowd.

The men looked first this way and then that way, each one hoping that his neighbor would take up a stone. But with the piercing eyes of Jesus upon them, each man remembered his own sin. No one dared throw a stone. The silence held. One by one, the men slunk away, leaving the woman before Jesus.

By and by he looked about. "Where are your accusers? Have they all gone? Does none of them condemn you?"

"No one, Teacher."

"Neither do I condemn you. Go, and sin no more."

When word was brought to the rulers that this plan, too, had failed to turn the crowds against Jesus, the high priest paced the floor in fury. The rulers sent others to question Jesus. And yet others. But the questioners found that Jesus was not the ignorant, foolish preacher they had supposed him to be. He dealt with their questions wisely, using them to teach the people, and leaving the questioners confused. With each failure to trap him, the anger of the leaders against him grew hotter. They were losing standing before the people, and Jesus was gaining in their favor. The situation was intolerable.

It was quieter in the Temple court now. Most of the people had gone to find food. Jesus and his disciples moved into an inner court. They had come to put their offerings into the trumpet-shaped receptacles, each one for a different purpose.

Before each receptacle sat a priest to check the offerings each contributor made. Around some receptacles stood men in rich robes, announcing in loud voices the amount of their contributions. Then, looking about proudly so that everyone might know of their generosity, they walked away. Ignoring these pompous ones, the eyes of Jesus were fixed upon a woman, poorly clad in the dress of a widow. The priest asked shortly about her coins and she answered in a low tone. With scant courtesy, the priest motioned her to put the coins into the box. But Jesus was deeply touched by the woman's gift.

"You saw the woman's gift. It was in the smallest coins that would be accepted. Yet I tell you that in the eyes of God she has put in a larger offering than all these others. For they have put in an offering out of their surplus money. But this woman has given all she had."

Their own turn had come for placing their gifts in the receptacles. Jesus and the disciples put in their offerings, and went out of the Temple.

CHAPTER XVIII

Outside the City

THE ENTHUSIASM of the crowds, the courageous action of Jesus in the Temple, had lifted the hopes of the disciples to a new height.

They had loved Jesus and they believed he was sent by God. At the same time they often had not understood him. Now their confidence was strong. Since the people had welcomed him, since he had so bravely asserted himself in the Temple, surely the time had come when he would publicly declare himself the leader Israel had so long expected.

And so, full of enthusiasm, the disciples started from the Temple to return to their lodgings outside the city. Looking back upon the great building, Peter exclaimed, "Look, Teacher, how glorious the Temple is!"

Jesus stopped and gazed long at the Temple. "Yes, a great building it is, indeed." After a moment he added, almost to himself, "Yet there will come a time when not one stone will be left upon another. It will be destroyed, all of it."

The disciples looked at one another, shocked by the words of Jesus, their hopes tumbling. These were not the words a victorious leader would speak about his capital city.

As they walked toward the Mount of Olives, the men

talked anxiously among themselves about what Jesus had said.

Judas' face was pale and strained. "Can he mean that Jerusalem will be destroyed? That the Romans will win?"

"He can't mean that," James declared. "He can't mean that."

"He is sent by God. Surely God will lead him to victory," John insisted hotly, as if to convince himself as well as the others.

But Peter was not convinced. "Jesus has never told us that he will lead Israel to victory. We all know that. And remember how he rebuked me when I told him he must not speak of suffering."

Simon nodded his agreement. "Yes, Peter. He has told us plainly that he is in danger, that he must suffer."

Judas listened, brooding. "Do you think his cause is lost, Peter? That he will really be arrested by the Romans?"

Peter spoke slowly. "I do not know, Judas. I do not know. He is God's chosen one. Of that I am sure. He says God will save us. And that I believe. Yet just as we think he is ready to declare himself the promised leader, he speaks of the destruction of the Temple. He says, too, that he will suffer. I—"

"He *is* in danger," Simon broke in positively. "Terrible danger."

"I will not believe that," James protested. "It cannot be. He is sent by God. God will protect him. He will lead Israel."

"Yes, he is the chosen one. God will protect him," John repeated emphatically.

"Instead of thinking about danger, we should be thinking about his triumph," James went on. "Remember what he did in the Temple. There are many of his sayings which we do not understand, and what he said about the Temple being destroyed is one of them. Let us forget it, and remember how the people cheered him, and how even the Sadducees were silenced by his replies to their questions."

"You are right, James," John agreed. "We should be thinking of Jesus' victory. And of our part in it," he added, as he turned to speak privately to his brother.

While the disciples were talking, Jesus was walking on alone. So much had happened. He was thinking of those who seemed to accept him, and of the leaders who even now were plotting against him. He knew that many of the people who were praising him were hoping that he would do wonders before them. He knew many others expected that he would become a national leader and free them from Rome. So few seemed to understand that there was only one way men could be saved. The way he had been sent by God to show them, the way of repenting of their sins and loving their neighbors and doing what was right and good.

As he climbed the slope of the Mount of Olives, Jesus looked down upon the city, the great city of his people. His heart was full of love and sorrow. "O Jerusalem, Jerusalem! I would have saved you, but you would not have it so."

On every hand he saw evidence of Roman power and Roman watchfulness. The great fortress of Antonia. The pacing soldiers. He knew that he might be arrested at any time. Instead of supporting him, the leaders of his people had turned against him and were likely to denounce him.

Upon what men, then, could he depend? The twelve? Even they had often shown that they did not understand. But they were the only men upon whom he could depend. He would help them all he could and trust the rest to God. For God's Kingdom would come!

For a moment he let his mind rest on the day when all men would be ready to enter the Kingdom of God, loving God and loving their neighbors. When there would be no more hungry children or suffering women; no more cruelty or hatred or greediness among men; no more conquerors and no more conquered; but all men helping each other with kindness and goodness and joy in their hearts. That was the Kingdom God had sent him to call man to enter. How glorious a Kingdom it would be!

Confidence and joy drove out discouragement, and Jesus prayed, "Our Father, thy Kingdom come on earth."

He turned to rejoin the disciples. James and John were just behind him, apart from the rest, primed with a question.

"Teacher, we want you to grant us a request," James began.

"What is the request, James?"

"When you come to power in the Kingdom of God, let us have the seats of honor, one on your right hand and one on your left hand."

Their eyes met those of Jesus without shifting. He saw that they were asking the favor in all sincerity. They expected him to be the great leader of their people, to exercise power as the kings of the nations of the world exercised power, to grant favors to his friends. Even now his own disciples were so far from understanding the Kingdom of God!

Jesus did not rebuke them. He led them to a place on the slope of the mountain overlooking the city. "You do not know what you are asking," he said.

The other disciples had heard the request. They were angry as they joined Jesus. Peter strode up to James and John. "Why do you ask for the chief places?" he demanded. "Have not I left everything to follow the Teacher? What is to be my reward? What right do you have to the chief places?"

Jesus' heart was heavy within him. Yet he spoke kindly. "Come," he said, "let us rest here on the mountain." The men threw themselves on the ground. When their faces, flushed with anger, were turned toward him, Jesus spoke to them.

"You know," he said, "that in the nations of the world the rulers have authority over other men. They order this one here and that one there, and show their power by overbearing manners." He paused a moment. "Do not let it be so among you," he went on. "Rather let the one who seeks to be greatest among you do the most for those who need him. I did not come to reign over men and be served by others. I came to help men and to call them to prepare for the Kingdom of God. A Kingdom where men will love God and live together as brothers, each one eager to do what is good for the others."

His eyes moved from one to another of his disciples, pleading with each one to understand. Then he asked, "Will you follow me in this?"

The disciples again were sorely puzzled. Jesus came from great triumphs in the Temple and talked to them not about his power, but about serving others!

Yet even in his confusion, Peter saw how Jesus loved them. His own love for the Teacher welled up and wiped out his anger. He would trust Jesus even if he did not understand. Ashamed now of his quarrel over rewards and position, once more he answered for all the disciples. "Yes, Teacher, we will follow you."

After a moment, Jesus spoke again. "I have told you that my life is in danger. I tell you again plainly that those who are against me have the power of life and death over my body." His voice became stronger, more confident. "But they have no power over God! And God sent me to prepare men for his Kingdom. Be not dismayed. Though I die, his Kingdom will come!"

Peter jumped up. All his fears for the safety of one he loved came rushing back upon him. "Teacher, let us escape while there is yet time. Let us go into the hills!"

Andrew joined Peter. "There are some Greeks here, eager to be your followers. Let us flee with them to their country," he urged.

Jesus shook his head. "No, Peter; no, Andrew; we will not flee. I will teach in the Temple what God wants me to teach. I will leave the results to God."

"But—" Peter began again.

"Nevertheless," Jesus went on, "I will not give myself into the power of those who seek my life. After I have taught in the Temple court during the day, we will come away each evening to this quiet place, and spend the night here in the olive grove. I shall use all the time I have."

And with this plan the disciples had to be content.

During the days that followed, Jesus went to the Temple where the crowds gathered round him in the outer court, hearing him gladly. Daily, too, the Sadducees and the Pharisees sought to trap him with questions. Because he answered them wisely, they could find nothing which would turn the people against him so that they might have him arrested without causing a tumult.

But Jesus knew that with each failure their anger was growing. He knew that the Pharisees were opposed to his teaching of God's love for all men, even the outcasts and sinners. They thought he was wrong when he said that man's need was more important than ceremonial laws. They were bitterly angry because he had criticized their pretense.

He knew that the Sadducees were willing to turn him over to the Roman soldiers because he had disturbed the Temple markets. He knew that the Romans were watching the crowds about him, ready to suspect him of stirring up a rebellion.

Those who opposed him were closing in upon him. He could win safety for himself if he would speak flatteringly of the leaders instead of calling them to repent of their sins and mend their ways. He could even now escape danger if he would accept the way of men instead of calling men to the way of God. But God had sent him to save men, not to flatter them. And so he continued to speak bravely.

The disciples were with him each day, marveling at his wisdom, feeling joy as the crowds heard him gladly. But they were anxious, too, about his safety. Simon, especially, was deeply worried. Whenever they passed a band of Roman soldiers, he felt as if his heart were in his throat. Whenever the crowds gathered, his eyes searched for spies among them.

James and John, though now they were ashamed of asking for first place, felt sure that Jesus would in some way overcome the danger in which they knew he stood. Just what he would do after the festival days were over, they could not forsee. Watching him as he taught in the Temple court, they talked about it.

"Do you suppose he will leave Jerusalem and return to Galilee as a teacher?" James asked.

"No, the people now expect more of him than that." John threw out his hands toward the people. "See how the people listen to him. No man ever had such power over the people. Yet he tells us he is not to be the leader of our nation!"

Judas came daily to the Temple with the others. He listened to what Jesus said. And he watched the people. He had become a follower of Jesus because he was moved by what he said and what he did. Judas was a patriot, yearning for the overthrow of Roman power. He had thought that Jesus would lead Israel against Rome.

But week after week, and month after month, Jesus had gone about the countryside and in the cities, talking about righteousness and helping the sick and making friends with the outcasts, rather than setting up a new government. Many had followed him, yes. But as Judas had looked at the crowds around him, he had wondered how many of the people would be useful in overthrowing Rome. All along Jesus had seemed to win the common people, but to offend the men who had influence and who might be useful to him in setting up a new government.

Then for a while, just before they started to Jerusalem and along the way, Judas' hopes had been high. It seemed as if there might be a turning point. But he knew now that the important men of Jerusalem would never accept Jesus as their leader. They had all turned against him. Daily in the Temple courts Judas saw his dreams fade of being a great man in the new nation.

He listened to the other disciples talking, and his bitterness grew. What weaklings they were! Halting between two sides, they asked one day for places of honor, and the next they scurried around trying to protect Jesus from danger. If he was to be the leader of the nation, Jesus did not need the protection of fishermen and taxgatherers. They seemed to be bound to the Teacher with some sort of cords. No matter how he disappointed them, they stayed with him.

Well, he, Judas, was not bound to any man. He was ready to be a loyal follower of the one who would lead his nation out of bondage. But he was not ready to spend the rest of his life traveling in poverty about the country with a man who seemed to think his most important work was to persuade the common people to love their neighbors.

Judas made up his mind. He would leave the band of disciples. He would stay with Jesus no longer. Jesus was not the leader Judas dreamed of.

Without saying anything to the others, he slipped out of the crowd and sat down in the shade of a great pillar of the Temple, thinking about where he would go and what he would do next. He must have fallen asleep, for suddenly he found that he was listening to men's voices on the other side of the pillar.

"We must delay no longer. The time has come to act," one was saying.

"Yes, but we still have the crowds to consider."

"We must take him at night, away from the crowds. Once he is arrested and the people see that he is a prisoner of Roman soldiers, they will leave him quickly enough. It is one thing to take a man forcibly from the court of the Temple where he is speaking words that please the crowd, and quite another to let the crowd see the man already in shackles, surrounded by an armed guard."

"True enough. I suppose your spies have found out where he stays at night?"

The other voice went on. "We had men looking for him last night. They did not find him. There are many places around Jerusalem where a man might stay, and we cannot rout out the pilgrims from every house where there are strangers. But we will find him soon."

"Time is important. We must have him out of the way before the great day of the Passover."

The voices were silent for a moment. Then one of them spoke again, questioningly.

"I suppose there is none of his band of followers who could be bribed to tell us where we might arrest him?"

"I doubt that there is one of them who is not bewitched by him as the crowds are. They seem all to be simple-minded men, who would follow a lost cause to the end."

"Well, there will be a meeting tonight at the high priest's house. Perhaps we shall hear there that he has been taken."

Long after the men had gone, Judas continued to sit back of the pillar, thinking. Why should he not tell the men where Jesus could be found? If he was not the leader, he was stirring up the hopes of the people falsely, just as he had stirred up Judas' own hopes. He was dangerous to Israel. He would be taken sooner or later, of that there was no doubt. And when he was taken, his disciples would probably be taken, too. The more he thought of it, the surer he was that he, Judas, was in danger, too. He did not want to find himself a prisoner of the Romans, accused of planning a revolution.

He made his decision. He would go to the palace of the high priest as soon as it was dark and tell the leaders where Jesus was spending the nights.

CHAPTER XIX

Under the Olive Trees

Each day as he was teaching, Jesus knew that the chief priests were seeking to find an excuse for having him arrested. He knew how powerful they were.

One evening as he left the Temple with the disciples, he saw spies following, watching every move. He said nothing about it to the others, but sent them on ahead. Later he went to their meeting place by a different route.

That night as he lay with his cloak around him on the rough ground of the olive grove, he thought of his disciples. There were so many things he wanted to say to them. They had had little time alone together during the last busy days. He knew they were troubled and anxious about the future.

The next morning he called Peter and John to him. "Go into the city to the house where we have been made welcome, and ask the man of the house to let us use his upstairs room for our supper. Then ask Philip and Judas to buy the provisions and prepare the meal for us, that we may eat it together."

Peter and John were pleased to have something definite to do. They had felt so restless. When they told the plan to Philip and Judas, Philip was glad to secure the provisions, and Judas, of necessity, went along to pay for what was purchased.

But his mind was in a turmoil. He had already been to the council of the chief priests. They had listened as he told them about the olive grove where Jesus spent the nights. And they had paid him for the information. Now, Jesus was planning to eat the supper in the city! Would he stay there overnight? Would the chief priests go to the olive grove and not find him whom they sought? Would they take their revenge on the one who had given them false information?

Judas knew he must get word to them of the change of plan. How could he do it? It seemed to him as if Philip would never be satisfied with the provisions. They went from one market to another before he was ready to make a purchase. When at last everything had been bought and taken to the room which the friend had made ready, Judas hurried away, leaving the others to prepare for the serving of the supper.

Once alone, he tried to think clearly. Finally he decided that he would have to tell the chief priests what had happened and suggest that they be ready to move, but wait until he came to them before setting out.

He hurried to the high priest's house and made this report, promising that he would slip away from the supper just as soon as he could after he had learned where Jesus would be that night. This plan the high priest had to accept.

The day was about over. Soon would come the sunset. The disciples felt it would not be wise to attract attention to the house where they were to eat supper; so they went quietly, entering in small groups.

As Judas came in, he asked Peter if he knew where they would spend the night.

"Why, in the olive grove, I am sure. No plans have been made to stay here. Besides, it would be dangerous."

When Jesus came with the others, they all took their places about the table. Following the custom, Jesus held the loaf of bread in his hands and asked the blessing and broke the loaf, giving a piece to each of his disciples. "As this bread is broken, so shall my body be broken," he said.

While the disciples were wondering why he spoke so, Jesus continued. "One of you is going to betray me. One who is eating with me."

The disciples gasped. Each one said, "Certainly, Teacher, I will never betray you!"

Looking about the table, Jesus saw in one face the guilt he knew would be there. But in the eleven others he saw only disbelief. And underneath all the misunderstandings he saw, too, that they loved him. He longed to comfort them, to help them be ready for the time of testing which he now was sure could be only a few hours away.

Judas knew that the high priest was waiting. What he was to do must be done quickly. While Jesus was talking, he slipped out and hurried through the night to the palace of the high priest, leaving Jesus with those who loved him.

"Do not be troubled," Jesus said to the disciples. "You believe in God, and you believe that God sent me. You believe that the words I speak, I speak not of myself, but that they are the words God wants me to speak.

"Whatever may happen, I cannot fail to do what God sent me to do: to tell men of God's love; to call them to repent of their sins, and do God's will. This is the only way they can be saved from the misery in which they live. This is the only way they can be ready to enter the Kingdom of God.

"I may not go with you much longer. You are to carry on the work I have been doing among men. Love one another as I have loved you. And God will not leave you alone. He will be with you, and comfort you and guide you.

"Let not your hearts be troubled. Remember, when I leave you, I go to my Father. After your sorrow will come joy."

The eleven disciples knew, now, that Jesus was telling them plainly that he was to be put to death. They did not know what to do.

"All of you will be afraid," Jesus was saying. "Though you love me, you will be hard-pressed and will leave me."

Peter cried out, "Teacher, I will never leave you!"

Jesus smiled sadly. "Do not be so sure of yourself, Peter. Before this night is over, before the cock crows at dawn, it may be easy for you to deny that you ever knew me."

But Peter protested more strongly. "Even if everybody else denies you, I will never deny you." And James and John and Andrew and Simon and all the others said the same.

It was growing late. They must return to the olive grove for the night. Jesus said the blessings for the end of the meal, and they sang together a hymn which they had all sung from boyhood. After that, they went out into the dark street and found their way back to the olive grove.

Jesus was sure, now, that the time had come. Soon he would be arrested and turned over to the Romans. He would be accused of stirring up the people, and he knew the cruel death which the Romans inflicted upon those whom they accused of revolt. His body shrank from the torture he saw before him. But more than this, he was suffering because he knew the evil purposes of men. In spite of all he had been able to do, they had not turned to God. Had his love not been enough?

"Sit here a while," he said to the disciples as they entered the grove. "I will go yonder and pray." Starting to move away from them, he paused a moment, then he asked Peter and James and John to go with him. "My heart is very sad," he said to them, and they saw the anguish in his face. "Stay near me." He went a little way from them and fell to the ground.

"Father, God. You can do all things. Save me from this cup of bitter suffering." Peter and James and John saw him lying

motionless on the ground. Their hearts were torn with love and sorrow.

Yet they were very weary. The days had been long. They had been confused and disturbed. The grove was very quiet. Their eyes were heavy. The words of Jesus as he prayed came faintly, as from a great distance. "I will not deny what you have sent me to make known to men. If it is necessary that I suffer at the hands of sinful men, thy will be done."

Jesus continued to pray. After a while, the agony passed. Though all men should turn against him, and though even his disciples should desert him, he would not be alone. For he knew that God was with him. God was his Father, and God would not forsake him. He had not failed. God's Kingdom would come! He could bear whatever he had to bear. He arose comforted and strengthened.

When he came to Peter and James and John, he found them asleep. "Could you not watch with me even one hour?" he asked softly. "How frail you are! Yet you do love me. And God will find a way to make you strong."

Then he woke them. They were rubbing their eyes, ashamed of having failed him, when lights began to flicker through the olive grove.

"What is that?" Peter became wide awake instantly. There was noise now of men marching and armor clanging. The torches were playing on the gray leaves of the olive trees, lifting them up as ovals of light against the gnarled, dark branches. The other disciples were all awake.

What Jesus had told them about his suffering flooded their minds. There could be no doubt about what was happening. They could see the helmet of the officer glinting in the light of the torches. Soldiers were coming to arrest Jesus.

"We have two swords here, Teacher," Peter whispered. "Shall we strike?"

"Put up your swords, Peter." The disciple stood irresolute.

Coming through the grove, the officer spoke to Judas in a low voice. "Which one is he? It is dark under the trees. And I saw the man only once."

"I will greet him," Judas promised. The officer ordered the soldiers to halt, and he and Judas went forward to the little group of men standing in the shadow of the trees. "Hail, Teacher," Judas said, standing before Jesus and giving him a ceremonial kiss upon the forehead.

"Judas!" Peter's cry of horror was drowned by the officer's quick command: "Take him and bind him!"

The soldiers seized Jesus and bound his hands together.

Until this moment the disciples had thought that it could not happen. They had believed that somehow God would protect Jesus from danger. But now they had seen him betrayed by one of themselves. They had seen him arrested. They felt lost and afraid—terribly afraid. At any time now the soldiers might turn upon them. For the moment the darkness protected them. This might be their last opportunity to escape. And so, their shadows merging with the shadows of the olive trees, the disciples fled into the night.

Jesus was left alone with the soldiers.

CHAPTER XX
The Place of the Trial

IT WAS late at night. The officer wished to deliver his prisoner to the authorities. He had been instructed to bring Jesus first to the palace of the high priest, where some members of the Sanhedrin were to be assembled. He ordered the soldiers to start at once.

Caiaphas had had no opportunity to speak to Jesus apart from the admiring multitude about him. He wanted to question the man before he was sent to Pilate, the Roman governor, for trial. He wanted to make sure that the case against him was one upon which Pilate could not fail to act.

As the members of the Sanhedrin waited for Jesus to be brought before them, they moved about restlessly. They were not sure that they could trust the information Judas had given them. They were not sure that the soldiers would be able to arrest the prophet, even if Judas did lead them to him. Secretly they thought perhaps Jesus did have some unusual powers, as the common people believed. He might be able to escape. Besides, they remembered that many of those whom they had sent to question the man had fallen under his spell.

Waiting impatiently, the members of the Sanhedrin went

over all they knew against Jesus. His new interpretation of the Law to put the needs of men before religious customs and ceremonies, his criticism of the scribes and Pharisees for their hypocrisy in making a show of their religious observances while failing to be concerned about others, his denunciation of the Temple markets, his claim that he was speaking for God—all these matters the members of the Sanhedrin considered. They afforded good reasons to the religious leaders for accusing the man of being a false prophet, a heretic, for silencing him and putting him out of the synagogues. But they did not afford strong reasons for asking the Romans to put him to death. And the Sadducees had determined that nothing less would be safe for them.

They did not wish to try Jesus themselves before the Sanhedrin. They did not wish to risk adding to the wrath of the people against them. It would be wiser to send him directly to the Roman governor for trial. The evidence against him must be evidence which the Romans would accept. And so they summed it up.

He had enlisted large groups of followers. He had been the cause of popular demonstrations in the streets. He had caused disturbances among the people. On these charges there was ample evidence. But more—spies had reported that he had said the Temple would be destroyed. Surely this was evidence that the man was thinking of a revolution, of battles! Even more serious, many of the people thought that he was more than an ordinary prophet. They thought he was the long-expected leader, one sent by God to save them from Rome. The Sadducees had reports from Galilee of efforts to make him king.

They made up their minds. The charge that they would bring before the Roman governor would be the charge that Jesus was a revolutionary, that he was stirring the people to revolt against Rome, claiming to be the king of the Jews.

Nicodemus listened to all the discussion, sick at heart. "But have you determined to bring all these charges to the Roman governor before you have yourselves examined the man? Does our Law condemn a man before he is heard and witnesses have been called?"

Caiaphas turned upon him. "Why do you continue to defend him? Do you wish to follow him yourself?" It was clear that the matter was already settled. Nicodemus spread his hands in a gesture of defeat. "I wish the matter to be handled in accordance with our own Law," he said.

"The matter will be handled correctly," Caiaphas retorted.

The sound of approaching soldiers came into the meeting room. From the window the members of the Sanhedrin saw the torches. Anxiously scanning the crowd in the flickering light, Caiaphas was relieved to see Jesus. "They have the prisoner," he announced, and hastened to take his seat.

The officer came to the door and formally reported that they had brought the prisoner for questioning. Caiaphas bade him bring the man before them. The soldier led Jesus into the room, his hands bound and tied with rope, but his face calm and unafraid. He made no protest against his arrest, but stood before the high priest in dignified silence.

The cold and unfriendly face of Caiaphas was touched with surprise as he noted the bearing of the prisoner. It was not that of a man before those who had the power of life or death over him; it was not that of a frightened culprit before his judges; it was not even that of a man of the common people before the great high priest. Rather, it was that of one of the ancient prophets of Israel standing as a man of God before the kings and fearlessly announcing the word of God. For a moment Caiaphas seemed to quail before the eyes of Jesus as Ahab had quailed before Elijah when the prophet denounced

the king for his evil doings. With an effort, he seemed to pull together his pride and authority.

The questioning began. The high priest sought to get from Jesus' own lips a statement that he had done or taught something which could be called an act of revolt against the Roman government.

He asked many questions about what Jesus taught, but his prisoner gave no answers. After a while Jesus looked straight into the eyes of the questioner. "I taught openly in the Temple court. Many of the men here heard what I said. They are witnesses. Why do you not ask them?"

One of the Temple guard, seeking to curry favor with the high priest, stepped forward and slapped the prisoner on the cheek. "Will you talk disrespectfully to the high priest?" he demanded.

Jesus turned to him. "If I have said anything that is not true, report what it is. But if I have spoken what is true, why do you smite me?"

The questioning continued. Finally Caiaphas leaned forward. "Answer me plainly. Did you tell the people that you are the one sent by God to deliver them?"

"I am sent by God," Jesus answered.

"This is blasphemy," the high priest cried.

Seeing he was to get no other confession from Jesus, Caiaphas determined, without more evidence, to send word to Pilate that Jesus claimed to be king of the Jews. He ended the examination abruptly. "Take charge of the prisoner until morning," he told the officer. "Then bring him to the praetorium before Pilate. The charges will be sent there."

The members of the Sanhedrin drew their robes about them lest they be defiled by touching a heretic and left the room, Caiaphas to go to his private quarters in the palace of the high priest, and the others to go to their homes.

Once more Jesus was alone with the soldiers. Having nothing to do until morning, they amused themselves by making sport of the prisoner, calling upon him to do some miracle for them. But Jesus answered them not at all. He seemed to withdraw from the soldiers, to close his ears to their taunts as he closed his eyes to their unfriendly faces. And so he seemed to find peace even in the midst of his tormentors.

While Jesus was in the palace of the high priest, the disciples were scattering, one going to one place to hide, another going somewhere else. But Peter and John checked themselves in their flight. Even in their terror they could not forget that they loved the Teacher.

"Let us follow him," Peter said.

John nodded. "If we keep in the shadows they may not see us. We can know at least where they have taken him."

So the two friends followed the torches through the night.

John noted the direction in which they were going. "They are taking him to the palace of Caiaphas. Perhaps I can get inside. I have often been there to sell fish. The porter may let me in."

"Will he not report you as one of the disciples?" Peter asked fearfully.

John shook his head. "I think not. He knows me only as a fisherman."

"I will stay outside. In the court," Peter decided.

As the two disciples came to the palace of the high priest, the soldiers were taking Jesus up the steps. The light of the torches showed him in the midst of them, a prisoner, with his hands bound. Peter and John shivered in the chilly night. How defenseless he looked! What could they do to help him, two fishermen against a band of soldiers? Two fishermen who might, themselves, be arrested on sight as his disciples?

After the soldiers had entered the palace, John went through the tradesmen's entrance. No questions were asked him, and he sought a place from which he could see what was happening. He could not get near enough to see into the room where the soldiers had taken Jesus, and could hear only scattered words of the high priest's questioning and of Jesus' answers.

Finally he saw the members of the Sanhedrin leave the room. And thereafter he hid miserably in his corner while he heard the loud voices of the soldiers taunting their prisoner.

In the courtyard below, Peter tried to keep his face in shadow as he warmed his hands by the fire. But as the servants passed back and forth, one of them noticed him, then looked more closely. "See here, aren't you one of the followers of this Jesus?"

Afraid for his very life, Peter answered hastily, "No. I do not even know the man."

But another servant came forward. "I have seen you with him! Just the other day in the Temple court."

"What are you talking about? I have never seen him," came Peter's terrified answer.

Now a servant girl joined the group. "Why, your accent gives you away. You are a Galilean, one of his followers, I am sure."

"No! No, I tell you. I do not know the man."

Even as Peter was speaking, the door of the high priest's palace was opened and the soldiers came out, the Teacher in the midst of them. Peter looked up, and Jesus' eyes fell upon his face. At that moment the crow of the cock came clearly through the gray dawn.

Then Peter remembered. He remembered how he had promised that he would lay down his life, rather than forsake Jesus. That he would never deny him. Could it be that it was only the evening before when they had been together in the upstairs room? Only the evening before that he had been so sure of himself? What a coward he was! What a miserable coward. He covered his face with his hands. Yet what could he do? He could not rescue the Teacher from the soldiers.

Wretched and full of shame, he slipped out of the courtyard while the servants were watching the soldiers. Alone in the dim morning, he wept bitterly. As the new day advanced, he crept away and hid himself in the house of a friend.

The soldiers, following their orders, led Jesus through the streets toward the praetorium, where Pilate, the Roman governor, was to hold the trial. The chief priests had advised him that they would send to him a prisoner charged with stirring up a revolt. They knew this charge would get prompt attention because the Romans had found the Jews ready for revolt, and were determined to deal harshly with any leader, to stamp out immediately any signs of trouble among the restless people.

The streets of Jerusalem were beginning to fill now with the pilgrims who had come to the Passover. As the crowd saw the soldiers leading a prisoner toward the praetorium, many of them started to follow from idle curiosity. They did not know who the prisoner was, as they fell in behind the soldiers. But as questions began to fly back and forth, they heard that it was Jesus.

Dismay filled the hearts of those who had believed in him. "Why, what has he done to anger the rulers?" they asked. "He taught men of God and his righteousness. He loved people and helped them. He did no evil. He did good." And they followed in deep distress.

But many of them were very much afraid. "He was sent by God," they whispered. "We are sure of that. But he has been arrested. Anyone who is for him now will be in danger. We must be careful. We do not dare to speak favorably of him."

Others were disappointed and angry. "I thought he was the one sent by God to deliver us. But he must have been just another imposter who has deceived us. Well, then, he is getting what he deserves. To stir up false hopes is wicked."

Some who had listened to Jesus but had not followed him spoke up. "Well, he did criticize the leaders. He did say that we should get ready for the Kingdom of God. Perhaps he was planning a revolution. Surely he was no prophet, or the soldiers could not have taken him so easily."

And so the crowd grew as the procession continued toward the praetorium, some sad, some frightened, some angry, some merely curious.

On a broad porch outside the palace, Pilate received the charges of the members of the Sanhedrin. They accused Jesus of stirring up the people to revolt. They said he claimed to be the king of the Jews.

When the soldiers brought the prisoner before Pilate, the governor looked at him in surprise. The man's face was not like that of most rebels, he thought. It was neither harsh nor fanatical. It was, indeed, a noble face. But Pilate was not a man to be impressed by a noble face in a prisoner accused of starting a revolt. So he addressed Jesus, immediately taking up the principal charge made against him.

"Are you the king of the Jews?"

Jesus knew why this charge had been made against him. He had not made any such claim for himself. Yet he knew, too, he could not say simply, "No." This would seem to Pilate and to these who accused him to be a denial that he was sent by God. This he would not deny. He was God's chosen one. And so he answered merely, "So you say."

Pilate wished to have a confession before he pronounced sentence. He picked up the charges. "It is said here that you advised the people not to pay taxes to Caesar, that you stirred them to revolt."

Jesus had not advised the people to refuse to pay taxes to Caesar. He had not called them to revolt against Rome. Quite the contrary. But the charges were made by men with whom the Romans wished to work. Jesus knew that nothing he said would be believed. And so he answered not a word.

Instead, he turned toward the crowd gathered to watch the trial. He saw the priests, unwilling to defile themselves by entering the palace of the governor before the feast day, but standing on the steps. They were watching eagerly, ready to bring forth more charges if need be. He saw some Pharisees and scribes, those who had opposed him for his teaching and who wished him silenced and put out of the synagogues. Some of them seemed satisfied with the way things were going. But others seemed disturbed, as if they wished now they had had no part in the matter. Certainly, not in bringing trumped-up charges of leading a revolt against Caesar. Yet none dared speak out to defend the prisoner.

Among the crowd Jesus saw men and women who had heard him gladly as he taught in Galilee, and as he taught in the court of the Temple. Many of them now were afraid for themselves. Some of them were expecting that he would perform some miracle to free himself from the soldiers, and they were disappointed because he did not. Some of them were seeing their hope crushed, their hope that he would deliver them from Rome, and their faces were dull. Some of them were indifferent to him, a rabble, eager only for excitement.

Here and there he saw faces full of love and compassion and sorrow. There was a man whose little child he had cured of his sickness. There was a man who had been bowed down by an awful sense of his sin and who had been given comfort and assurance of God's love and forgiveness. There were the women who had been with him in Galilee: Mary Magdalene, Salome, and Joanna, and other women to whom he had brought hope and healing and comfort. These had not deserted him. He looked over the crowd again. No, the disciples were not there. Not one of them.

Pilate again scanned the charges, and saw that Jesus was from Galilee, the province over which Herod Antipas had been placed as king by the Romans. Since the case seemed unlike the usual cases of revolt, Pilate decided to send the prisoner to Herod for examination before he pronounced sentence. Herod was near by, having come to Jerusalem for the festival; so the soldiers were ordered to take Jesus at once to him.

For a long time Herod had wished to see Jesus. The reports he had had of him from his spies had frightened the puppet king. He knew his throne was not secure and he was jealous and afraid.

Now as Jesus came before him, bound and surrounded by Roman soldiers, Herod rubbed his hands together in evil satisfaction.

"So you would take my throne? You would be king of the Jews? We shall, indeed, make you king!" He laughed coarsely and called for a purple robe and a scepter, ordering the king's robe draped about the prisoner's shoulders and the scepter placed in his hands. When the king demanded a crown, the soldiers made a wreath from the branches of a thorn tree and placed it on Jesus' head. Then Herod mocked him. "Hail, king of the Jews!" And all the soldiers shouted in derision, "Hail, king of the Jews!"

Jesus made no response to the mockery. Herod soon grew impatient for fresh excitement, and sent the prisoner back to Pilate's court.

Jesus stood again before the Roman governor. But though he looked his judge steadily in the face, he said not another word. He knew the result of the trial was already decided.

Pilate did not require much evidence against a man accused of plotting against the government. A revolution in his territory would very likely mean that he would be removed from office. After all, the members of the Sanhedrin had said Jesus claimed to be king of the Jews. Herod had long thought that the man was dangerous. This was evidence enough. It was safer for the Roman governor to condemn a man who was innocent than to let go one who might be guilty of starting a revolt. So Pilate turned impatiently from a prisoner who refused to speak in his own defense.

"Take him away," he said to the soldiers.

Revolt against the government was considered the most serious of crimes, and the penalty was death. The punishment for a man of a subject people was the most terrible death that could be inflicted. To be judged guilty of revolt against Rome meant crucifixion. When a prisoner had been condemned to be crucified, he had no more protection. There was no mercy for him. No mercy at all.

Now the soldiers made sport of Jesus. Some of the people in the crowd, fearful lest someone had seen them with Jesus and might accuse them of helping plan a revolt to make him king, began shouting, "We have no king but Caesar! We have no king but Caesar!"

The soldiers tired of their sport. They took off the bright cloak, stripped Jesus, and beat him, as provided by Roman law, with a scourge of thongs. Then they put his own cloak back upon him, and led him away to be crucified.

CHAPTER XXI

Calvary

IT WAS the custom to place a sign over the cross on which a man was to be crucified, naming his offense. Pilate gave orders that a sign should be made for the cross of Jesus bearing the words, "The king of the Jews." The Sadducees asked to have it changed to read, "He says he is the king of the Jews." But Pilate refused. "What I have written, I have written," he said coldly, and returned to his house.

To announce that Jesus had been condemned to be crucified and to make the horrors of the punishment a warning to all others, the prisoner was led through the city carrying his own cross. A crowd followed from the praetorium through the streets of Jerusalem toward a hill outside the city. Some of those who only the day before had gathered around Jesus in the Temple court, hanging on his words, praising his courage, seeking his help, now joined the careless mob jeering at him, as he staggered under the weight of the cross.

But not everyone jeered. Faithful followers were on the road, the women sobbing openly. Many a good man and woman in Jerusalem who, for fear, did not dare defend him openly, wept for him in secret. And others wept for themselves and for their country, feeling hopeless and lost.

Thus the procession came to a rocky hill, just off the road, outside the city walls. Two criminals had been brought by other soldiers to be put to death at the same time. On the wayside hill, three crosses were raised. There they crucified Jesus between two criminals. The soldiers mocked him, and cast lots to see who would win his clothes. And the passersby called out taunts to him. "If you are the one sent by God, why do you not save yourself?"

The criminals were cursing their tormentors. But Jesus uttered no words of abuse.

The Roman officer in charge had seen many men in torture upon a cross. He had never before known one to suffer crucifixion without screaming curses. Seeing that Jesus was speaking, he listened intently. The words stunned him. For in his agony, Jesus was saying, "Father, forgive them, for they know not what they do."

The soldier backed away. "Surely this man was no criminal!" he whispered. "He was a righteous man sent by God."

A heavy storm came up, and the sky grew dark as night. The voice from the cross came again through the darkness. "It is finished." The Roman officer, trembling, hid his face. It was terrible to see any man die on a cross. To know that he had crucified an innocent man was unbearable.

But he had his position to think of. He must not seem before his soldiers and the people to be a weakling, unnerved by the sight of a crucifixion. With a great effort he straightened up and became once more the Roman captain.

Standing far from the cross to avoid the rough soldiers and the mocking crowds were the women who had ministered to Jesus in Galilee and who had followed him along the road from Jerusalem. They heard his cry, and knew that his sufferings were over.

There was one last service which they could do for him.

They could prepare his body for burial. While they were hesitating to approach the soldiers, they saw two men who looked as if they were persons of importance speak to the Roman captain. The captain gave a brief command and the soldiers took down the cross of Jesus and the men ordered the body taken away. The two women followed at a distance.

Coming to a garden not far away, the men made ready a new tomb which had been cut out of the rock. They wrapped the body of Jesus in linen garments and laid it in the tomb. Then they rolled up a large stone to cover the opening and went away.

As the men passed near the place where the women were standing, their faces could be seen more clearly. The women recognized them as Joseph of Arimathea and Nicodemus the Pharisee, two men of influence who, some said, were secretly followers of Jesus.

"What cowards they were!" Mary Magdalene said.

"Men of influence such as they are might have saved Jesus if they had not been afraid to say openly that they were his followers," Salome added, more in sorrow than in reproach.

"And yet," Mary Magdalene went on slowly, as if trying to put strange thoughts into words, "could anything have saved him?"

"You mean—"

"Jesus would always have called them to repent of their sins, these proud men of power who refused to do the will of God. And they would always have fought him."

Salome broke into fresh weeping. "But God could have saved him."

"Yes, God could have saved him. It is past our understanding, Salome. Yet I know he is not as other men are. I know what he did for me. Perhaps, even yet—" Her voice trailed off into nothingness as she stood looking at the tomb where the body of Jesus had been laid. Then the women heard from the distance the trumpet announcing the beginning of the Sabbath, and they hurried home.

When the Sabbath was past, the women came early in the morning to the place where they had seen the body of Jesus laid in the tomb. As they came near, they stopped suddenly. The stone had been rolled away. What had happened? They walked slowly to the tomb. Stooping, they looked in. The tomb was empty. They looked at one another in fear.

"Has someone stolen the body?" Salome whispered, trembling.

Gradually fear gave place to wonder. Mary Magdalene looked again toward the empty tomb.

"Or could it be—could it be that he is alive?" Her face was shining. "Not dead, but alive!"

CHAPTER XXII

To All the World

DURING the trial and crucifixion of Jesus, the disciples had been scattered, terrified, grief-stricken, bitterly ashamed. Most of them had remained hidden, not knowing what had happened.

"There was never a man so vile as I," Peter moaned, tossing on the pallet spread for him in the home of a trusted friend who had been willing to hide him. "I loved him, yet I said I did not know him. He needed me, and I thought only of my own worthless life."

"Do not torment yourself, Peter," James said wearily. "We all were cowards." He began pacing the floor. "Yet what could we have done? What could we have done that would have saved him?"

Peter was paying little attention to James's words. His own thoughts were tormenting him. "He looked at me. He knew me for what I was. A man who boasted of his bravery when his friend was in no danger, and who turned traitor when danger came near."

The memory was more than he could bear, and Peter beat his fists upon the floor helplessly.

After a while he lifted his head. "And yet, James," he

said wonderingly, "there was no reproach in his look. It was almost as if he spoke to me and said he forgave me."

James nodded. "He would forgive us. He forgave all our boasting, our seeking for first place. He would forgive us even for deserting him in his hour of need."

"What do you suppose they did to him?" Peter jumped up. "I must know! Hiding here behind locked doors when he is in the hands of those who would—"

He broke off suddenly as someone knocked at the door. He was beyond fear now. He strode to the door, unbolted it, and threw it open. Andrew and Simon, red-eyed from weeping and lack of sleep, stumbled inside. Pulling the door shut, Simon threw the bolt. The faces of James and Peter told him they did not know.

"You have not heard, then?" he began.

"Where is he? What have they done to him?" Peter demanded.

Simon turned to James. "Your mother was there, James. She and the other women stayed to the end."

"Stayed? The end?" Peter was beside himself. He clutched Simon by the arm. "Tell me!"

And so Simon told them that Salome, the mother of James and John, had found his hiding place and had reported to him all she had seen of the trial and the crucifixion and the burial in the garden tomb.

"She is at the home of her sister now, but as soon as the Sabbath is past, she and the other women will visit the tomb," he finished.

The words came to Peter and James as if they were heavy blows upon their bodies. They staggered and fell upon their pallets. Overwhelmed with grief, they could not speak.

Later in the day, John joined them. Then Thomas and Nathaniel came.

The night dragged on. Exhausted, they slept fitfully. The Sabbath came and went. They ate a little dry bread. Another night. Another morning.

There was someone at the door. Opening it cautiously, James saw his mother, Salome, and Mary Magdalene. Their faces were full of light.

Before any questions could be asked, they were telling the disciples about the empty tomb. But the disciples thought the women's grief must have made them ill.

"Come. Come with us," Mary Magdalene urged them. "Let us show you."

So Peter and John went with the women to the garden. They saw the empty tomb. But they did not know what to make of it. Perhaps, they thought, the women had been mistaken about seeing Jesus buried there.

They returned to the other disciples, bewildered.

A few mornings later, Peter rose early. "I am going back to Galilee," he announced. "The fishing boats are still by the sea. I am going back to fishing."

Andrew was relieved to hear Peter once more making plans. "I will go with you," he said. As they started, the others followed, returning to their own part of the country.

Walking over the familiar road, the disciples were reminded of Jesus at every step of the way.

"It was just here, as we were going to Jerusalem, that he told us he would suffer, and we would not believe him," Peter said.

"And it was here," James remembered with bitter shame, "that you and I, John, asked him to give us first place when he came to power."

"And it was here," Andrew said, "that he told the story of the forgiving father."

John was deep in thought. "He told us that God would

forgive us as the father forgave the prodigal son. Could God forgive us even this? That we denied Jesus?"

"Yes, John, God will forgive even that." Peter spoke with sudden conviction. "I saw forgiveness in the face of Jesus himself."

"To be forgiven! Yes, I can believe that. But what are we to do?" Thomas asked.

Andrew spoke hesitatingly. "He told us what to do when he sent us out to the villages. Do you suppose we should try now to do what he told us to do then?"

John looked hopeful for a moment, then doubtful. "But then he was here. We could come to him for help. If only he was with us now!"

The next day they were back in Galilee. Here it seemed almost impossible to think that Jesus was not with them. There was not a road which they had not traveled with him, scarcely a town where they had not heard him teach.

And so, remembering Jesus, longing for him, the disciples came again to Capernaum.

That very evening the four fishermen went down to the Sea of Galilee, and made ready the boat they had left beached there. Thomas and Simon and Nathaniel went with them to the shore, and helped mend the nets and launch the boat. When the boat was ready to go out onto the sea, the four fishermen asked the others to go along.

All night they fished. But they had little to show for their labor. The catch was very poor. As dawn was breaking they started back to shore.

Peter mused aloud. "That other night when we had caught nothing and came in to shore, we found Jesus there, waiting for us."

"It was the very day he called us to be disciples," John remembered. "He said we should fish for men."

They were all silent, the four fishermen living again that day which seemed so long ago.

"He said over and over that we should carry on his work," Peter went on. "But how can we? We have all been such cowards. I, who bragged the most, have been the basest coward of us all."

Thomas was shaking his head. "What is it we could do? Even if we dared work as his disciples? He has died. To tell men to follow him now would be to tell men to prepare to die."

Peter was wrapped in thought as he guided the boat through the gray dawn. "I cannot believe he is dead. He was so alive! He knew that God had sent him to men. He knew that God's Reign would come! How could he die?"

Simon nodded as Peter spoke. "I know, Peter. Yet we misunderstood him so. Our minds were so dull. If only he were here now! After these awful days we might be ready to understand him."

They could see the dim shore now, only a little way ahead. It seemed that someone was walking there. The men were looking forward eagerly. The memory of that other morning was vivid before them. Could it be? Could it be that Jesus was there again? That he had heard the cry of their hearts and had come again to comfort and reassure them?

They brought the boat to shore. A fire was burning and fish and bread were cooking. Worn out and hungry, the disciples ate and were refreshed. And Jesus was there with them by the seaside as he had been with them so many times. Jesus was with them! He was not dead, but alive!

They heard the words he spoke. "Peace I give to you. As God has sent me forth, so I send you forth. Teach men what I have taught you: to repent of their sins, to love God and to love their neighbors. So God's Kingdom will come."

The disciples were quiet, full of awe, not able to speak. Then came the direct question.

"Peter, do you love me?"

"You know all things about me, Teacher. You know that I love you."

"Then feed my sheep."

Peter remembered the story Jesus had told of the good shepherd who would risk his very life to rescue even one lost lamb. At last he understood what Jesus had so often shown him. He knew now what it was Jesus wanted him to do. It was to look after people who needed him, as a shepherd looks after his sheep. It was to tell people the good news Jesus had brought: that God loves each one of them, even the least; that he is waiting to forgive them their sins, as a father waits to forgive a runaway son. It was to help people know that Jesus had, indeed, come to save them, to show them that God will make them over into good men and help them to be ready to take their place in the Kingdom of God.

Again they heard the words of Jesus: "Go and make disciples of all peoples everywhere and teach them all that I have taught you. My work, now, I commit to you. And I shall be with you all the time, even to the end of the world."

How different it was to be from what the disciples had once thought! No earthly kingdom, no positions of power, no armies of marching men to lead against other armies. Instead, they were to help all who needed them, knowing the time would come when all men of all nations would be brought into the Kingdom of God. When all men would love one another, help one another, serve God together as Jesus had taught them.

The faces of the disciples were filled with wonder and great joy. Jesus was with them, now, by the sea. He would always be with them. He had forgiven them their cowardice

and their dullness of understanding. He had trusted his work to them. Comfort and courage were flowing into their lives, bringing strength to do the work Jesus was leaving to them.

Once more the fishermen's boat was turned over on the land, and the fishing nets thrown over it to dry. There was so much the disciples must do! So many people to whom to tell the good news!

And once more as they turned to leave the seashore the words came to them.

"Do you love me?"

"You know us altogether, Teacher. You know we love you."

"Then feed my sheep."

PRINTED IN U.S.A.